ADVANCE PRAISE FOR NEVER FLY SOLO

"*Never Fly Solo* not only is a great reminder that we all need the help and support of others in our pursuit of success but also acts as a guidebook for how we can make it happen."

> —*Larry Winget, television personality and* New York Times *bestselling author of* It's Called Work for a Reason

"*Never Fly Solo* is exactly what business leaders need today to build trust both internally and with their customers. A compelling read, it's a timely reminder of the core values that make for an effective organization: integrity, accountability, and a commitment to service."

> —*Jeff Duckworth, Executive VP and* *Head of Sales, John Hancock Funds*

"*Never Fly Solo* is a must-read for anyone seeking personal and team excellence. This accomplished aviator and seasoned entrepreneur shares insights that you can put to work immediately for higher performance. This book will not only reinforce your team spirit but also inspire new levels of courage when dealing with adversity. Don't miss this one!"

> —*Don Hutson, coauthor of the* New York Times *#1 bestseller* The One Minute Entrepreneur

"Great advice for anyone who wants to communicate and connect on a deeper level—particularly leaders tempted to view themselves as 'self-made success stories.' Highly recommended to build a team culture."

> —*Dianna Booher,* *author of* The Voice of Authority: 10 Communication Strategies Every Leader Needs to Know

"If you want to be a leader and make an impact on the world, you can't do it alone. You need your wingmen, your team. The only way to be a leader that attracts wingmen is to be a person of integrity, passion, and authenticity. *Never Fly Solo* gives you the tools you need to be that leader."

> —*Chris Widener,* *author of* The Art of Influence

"A must-read that provides a simple yet powerful set of guidelines to help build leadership qualities and character in all facets of life."

—*Matthew Walsh,*
CEO of Walsh Construction

"Finally, an aviation-based leadership book that focuses on what really matters in the heat of battle—the trust you have in your wingmen."

—*Brigadier General Steve Ritchie,*
U.S. Air Force Retired,
the only Air Force Pilot Ace
of the Vietnam War

"When you're ready to chase a challenge, *Never Fly Solo* will help you win. This book is packed with powerful insights on building trust and motivation and leading a team."

—*Randy Gage,*
author of Prosperity Mind

"In these challenging economic times, Waldo's book serves as a bold wake-up call to the business world that trust and service are critical to maintaining a competitive advantage in the marketplace."

—*Bill Bartmann,*
billionaire business coach

"*Never Fly Solo* is authentic and relevant and told from the perspective of a real-world warrior with a heart. It's a wonderful gift you should share with those you care about."

—*Brendon Burchard,*
author of Life's Golden Ticket

"Waldo effectively captures the critical leadership attributes necessary to succeed when adversity and change strike. In this tough economy, I can't think of a more relevant business book."

—*Jeffrey Fox, bestselling author of*
Rain: What a Paperboy Learned About
Business *and* How to Become CEO

★★★★★

NEVER
FLY
SOLO

★ ★ ★ ★ ★

NEVER FLY SOLO

Lead with Courage, Build Trusting Partnerships, and Reach New Heights in Business

Lt. Col. Rob "Waldo" Waldman

New York   Chicago   San Francisco   Lisbon   London   Madrid   Mexico City
Milan   New Delhi   San Juan   Seoul   Singapore   Sydney   Toronto

Library of Congress Cataloging-in-Publication Data

Waldman, Rob.
    Never fly solo: lead with courage, build trusting partnerships and reach new
heights in business / by Rob "Waldo" Waldman.
        p.   cm.
    Includes index.
    ISBN: 978-0-07-163706-0
    1. Success in business.   2. Leadership.   3. Partnership.
4. Management.

    HF5386 .W159   2010
    658.4'092—dc22   2009042900

7 8 9 10 11 12 13 14 15 16 17 18 19 20 21 QFR/QFR 1 5 4 3

ISBN 978-0-07-163706-0
MHID   0-07-163706-0

McGraw-Hill books are available at special quantity discounts to use as
premiums and sales promotions or for use in corporate training programs.
To contact a representative, please e-mail us at bulksales@mcgraw-hill.com.

The content of this book is not endorsed by nor does it constitute official policy of the
U.S. Department of Defense or the U.S. Air Force.

To my twin brother, Dave . . . my ultimate wingman

CONTENTS

ACKNOWLEDGMENTS

WRITING THIS BOOK has undoubtedly been one of the toughest missions of my life. It has also been one of the most rewarding. If not for my wingmen who encouraged me to "push it up" and take action, this book would never have seen print. This book is a testament to the power of having wingmen in your life.

First, I have to thank my amazingly supportive family, who have been with me every step of the way. They have been the wind beneath my wings. Special thanks go to my twin brother, Dave, to whom this book is dedicated. How lucky I've been to have you on my wing always! Who could ask for a greater blessing? Whether you realized it or not, you've lifted me in too many ways to list here, giving me the thrust to take off on my most challenging missions. I love you very much.

To my parents, Leonard and Sylvia: thank you for being the best "wing mom" and "wing dad" a guy could ask for. Your unconditional love, support, and inspiration mean more to me than words on paper can express. To Leslie and Steven: thank you for being such great role models for me. I hope I can one day be a parent like you. I love you all.

For their wisdom and support in developing this book, I would like to extend my sincerest gratitude to:

- My wingmen at the National Speakers Association, who have been "checking my six" since I started speaking professionally. Thank you for being part of my extended family. Ken Futch and Gene Griessman, you have been great friends and mentors. Thank you for inspiring me to "push it up."

- My coaches, informal mentors, and unsung heroes: Jim Cathcart, Max Dixon, Lou Heckler, Jeffrey Gitomer, Bill Treasurer, David Greenberg, Rick Stark, Lee Coe, Archie Deese, Dick Biggs, Alex Mandossian, Jim Eberle, Max Howard, Jim Feldman, Terry Brock, Chris Hoskin, Steven Roddy, Laura Grierson, Marty Grunder, Sam Silverstein, Mike Tasner, Rick Searfoss, and countless others who worked behind the scenes to help me fly.

- My mastermind group: Dan Thurmon, Tim Gard, and Mike Rayburn. You guys have been awesome, and I appreciate all your advice and encouragement. Thanks for checking my six.

- Dan Seidman. There is no other person who helped me more with this book. You are everything a wingman stands for. Thank you for your commitment, patience, and insights.

- Chris Widener, family man, leader, and friend. Thanks for the lifts and the laughs.

- Mark Sanborn. You practice what you preach. Thank you for being a wing giver.

- Dianna Booher. Thank you for your professional book coaching and for going above and beyond with your advice and feedback.

- Kathy Fletcher. I couldn't ask for a better right-hand wingman to keep me focused and on target. I appreciate beyond words your attention to detail and commitment. You have been a blessing to me, both personally and professionally.

- Jeffrey "Flash" Gordon. I'm so grateful that you showed up in my formation. I look forward to exploring new targets with you.
- My wonderfully talented graphic designer, Lisa Reynolds. You showed up out of the blue and gave unconditionally from day one. I appreciate your creative insights and, most of all, your character. You are a true professional.
- My editing and creative wingmen at McGraw-Hill, who believed in me and the wingman philosophy from the start: Knox Huston, for all your vector corrections and encouragement; Mary Glenn, for being a peerless flight lead; and Gaya Vinay, Ann Pryor, Susan Moore, and all the other staff who were wingmen on this book. Thank you for your passion about this project.
- Kevin Small. Your expert advice and guidance helped make this book a reality. Thank you.
- My business attorney, Frank Benjamin. When the turbulence came, you guided me to clearer skies. Thanks for your friendship and amazing skill.
- My talented publicist, Mark Fortier, for your expertise and generous advice.
- Phil Parker, photographer extraordinaire and all-around stellar human being. Thanks for helping put a face on the cover of this book.
- My IT wingman, Randy Pelkey. Thanks for keeping me airborne when the computer missiles were flying.
- My top gun editor, Michael Carr, for coming through last minute and doing some amazing editing on the final manuscript. The missiles were coming, and you helped me dodge them!

- My clients, who bless me with the opportunity to share my wingman message of courage and mutual support to their teams.
- My best friends in the world, Al Wansky and Mark Wiltchik. You helped shape who I am today. The major victories in my life were due, in large part, to you. When I call out "Mayday!" you are always there. I am so blessed to have you in my life.
- Dana Wilson. Thank you for your easy silence and your angel wings.
- My wingmen from the 79th Fighter Squadron "Tigers" at Shaw Air Force Base, South Carolina, and the 35th Fighter Squadron "Pantons" at Kunsan Air Base, South Korea. What a privilege it was to serve with you all. The memories will be with me forever.
- My classmates and faculty from the U.S. Air Force Academy, past, present, and future. There is no finer institution training our country's leaders. I am honored to be a graduate and an admissions liaison officer for this amazing school.
- My flight lead: God.

And, finally, to the veterans around the world who are warriors for peace and freedom. You lent your country your wings, and some of you even sacrificed them. We cannot and will not forget you. You are real-world wingmen who live the principles of courage, commitment, and service. God bless you and your families.

INTRODUCTION

THE JOURNEY TOWARD earning my wings in life began long
before I earned my Air Force wings. The youngest of four
children, I was raised on Long Island, New York, in a very
competitive middle-class family of overachievers, led by the
first "general" I ever served with: my overprotective mother.
Sylvia (or "Silly," as we lovingly called her) had my conserva-
tive, workaholic dad, Lenny, as her wingman. They both grew
up dirt poor in Brooklyn, with no real opportunity to go to
college. My dad served eight years in the Navy before he
became an airplane mechanic. My mom stayed home and
raised the kids.

Together they taught my sister, two brothers, and me the
value of hard work, education, integrity, compassion, and,
most of all, family. These were the greatest gifts any parents
could give their children. And while I didn't know it then,
they were the first wingmen who had a major impact on my
life. My "wing mom" and "wing dad" were my first instructor pilots, and I love them dearly.

The other very special wingman in my life is my identical
twin brother, Dave. While we are different in many respects
and each march to our own drummer, Dave and I give each
other something irreplaceable: mutual support. We seldom
experienced an obstacle, adversity, or victory alone. With
Dave on my wing, I've never had to fly solo, and to this day
there is no one I trust more.

When I was eight, my childhood and life path changed dramatically the day my dad took Dave and me to work with him at Kennedy Airport in Queens. I jumped onto the concrete tarmac and grinned with enthusiasm as the roar of jet engines blasted my eardrums. I gazed into the sky, mesmerized by the floating metal birds taking off, as I breathed in the intoxicating scent of burning jet fuel for the first time.

Then my dad sat me in the cockpit of a real Boeing 747 jumbo jet. I fiddled with the switches and was fascinated with all the dials and instruments.

"What's this place for, Dad?" I asked.

"This is the cockpit, Robert. It's where the pilot *flies* the plane."

And right then and there, something clicked, and my life path was clear to me. I didn't want to fix planes like my dad did—I wanted to *fly* them!

Years later, when it came time for me to pick a college, the Air Force Academy seemed the logical choice. I had always thrived on challenge, and the thought of becoming a fighter pilot and officer in the Air Force really excited me. After the long and tedious application process, I was offered an appointment. It was one of the happiest moments of my life.

To ensure that I was making the right choice about my future, I decided to take a guided tour of the academy with Mom and Dad on my wing. We entered the huge gymnasium with its beautiful Olympic-size swimming pool. And in the distance was what would become my nemesis my entire freshman year: a thirty-three-foot high diving board.

I slowly pointed to the diving board, and the hair stood up on the back of my neck as I asked the tour guide, "Uh, sir? Do we have to jump off that thing?"

"Absolutely," he replied. "As a matter of fact, you can't graduate from the academy unless you complete water survival training and jump off that diving board."

My mom said I turned pale as a ghost.

Unbeknownst to the academy, I had a tremendous fear of heights growing up. I was the kid at the local swimming pool who couldn't even muster the courage to jump off the ten-foot diving board. And believe it or not, I'm also a (recovering) claustrophobe! I used to be barely able to go inside a closet for longer than ten seconds without having a panic attack.

Eventually, I overcame these fears to become a decorated fighter pilot with sixty-five combat missions in Iraq and Serbia. And while I may have flown these missions strapped into the cockpit of a single-seat F-16, I was never flying solo.

We all have fears, doubts, and self-limiting beliefs that hold us back from breaking the performance barrier in our work and our lives. Yet it's the relationships we build and the people whom we trust that give use the courage to take risks and make ourselves better.

I learned about trust with my classmates while struggling through those four brutal years at the academy. Then I put that trust to use in the real world with my squadron mates while flying six-hour night combat missions over Iraq.

Trust. That's what this book is about. It's not about combat or how to apply jet-fighter tactics to beat the competition. It is, above all else, about building trust in yourself and then building trusting relationships with others. These trusted partners, male or female, are your wingmen.

My mission in *Never Fly Solo* is to give you a flight plan that, if followed, will help you "earn your wings"—overcome your fears, build trusting partnerships, and reach new heights of success.

It won't be easy. Growth seldom is. It will involve risk, courage, and commitment. But I guarantee you, the journey will be well worth it.

If not for the trust I had in my wingmen, and my commitment to conquer my fears, I would never have graduated from the Air Force Academy or had those silver Air Force pilot's wings pinned to my chest. I would not have had the opportunity to travel the world, break the sound barrier in an F-16, or teach dozens of people how to fly jets. Nor would I have endured yearlong remote tours of duty in Korea, deployments to the sweltering Saudi Arabian desert, horrific panic attacks at 20,000 feet in the night skies of Iraq, or surface-to-air missile launches. After all, it takes courage to step outside your comfort zone and pursue your passions.

It was the courage I learned in the Air Force that gave me the courage to *leave* the Air Force. I left behind a secure military career and flew into very unfamiliar territory. Armed with an M.B.A. but no real-world business experience, I entered the corporate world and eventually started my own consulting business. It was a huge risk, and I failed countless times while struggling to adapt to this new mission. What made the difference for me were the wingmen who had my back and kept me on target. Just as in combat, I was never flying solo.

My point? That risk has its rewards as well as its challenges. To succeed, you not only have to be willing to deal with the missiles en route to the target, but you also need trusting partners on your wing—partners who will *look out for you and help you perform at your best.*

Every day, new missiles are launched. The changing economy, budget cuts, layoffs, turnover, health challenges, family issues—they're all part of life. And in the midst of these challenges, you may find yourself at a crossroads in your life, facing some very serious decisions and commitments. Will you leave your current job and start a new career? Will you ask for that promotion? Are you going to take on that new leadership role? Can you *ever* find a job that gives you fulfillment and meaning? When the tough times come, will you have the support necessary to make it through?

It is my fervent hope that *Never Fly Solo* will provide the tools and tactics that give you the thrust necessary to meet these challenges head-on. I want you to be mission-ready when the missiles come and to defeat them with confidence and courage. And I want you to do it with honor and integrity. More than ever, the world needs people who embrace these core values. It needs wingmen who will stand up and do the right thing every time.

Most important, I want you to know that you don't have to do it on your own—in fact, contrary to the American image of the maverick, solo-flying entrepreneur, you *shouldn't*. You have the choice to fly with others and let them be a part of your formation for success.

For now, I ask only that you trust me to fly this mission on your wing. Let me be your wingman and help lead you to the target. I'll have your back, and I won't leave you behind.

So strap in, fire up your engine, and prepare to release the brakes. We've got a mission to accomplish.

It's time to *push it up*!

THE WINGMAN CREDO

I AM YOUR WINGMAN

YOU CAN COUNT ON ME

INTEGRITY, SERVICE, AND COURAGE ARE AT THE CORE OF ALL I DO

I AM COMMITTED TO EXCELLENCE, ACCOUNTABLE FOR RESULTS, AND TRUSTWORTHY

MISSION-READY AND FOCUSED, I AM ALWAYS PREPARED

I WILL LEND YOU MY WINGS IN THE HEAT OF BATTLE

LEADER. CONFIDANTE. PARTNER

I WILL NEVER LEAVE YOU BEHIND

AND I WILL NEVER LET YOU FLY SOLO.

1

Push It Up!

Attitude Plus Action Determines Altitude

THE BRIEFING ROOM hums with the nervous chatter of thirty-three trainees awaiting their official in-briefing. We're newly commissioned second lieutenants, stationed at Williams Air Force Base in the scorching heat of a Phoenix summer. The next twelve months are known as UPT—undergraduate pilot training—and the only thing any of us can think about is jumping into the Cessna T-37 "Tweet" twin-engine jet trainer and pushing up the throttles. The future is finally beginning.

Maj. Jerry Free, the flight commander of "Scat Pack" flight (part of the 98th Flying Training Squadron), walks in the door. Capt. R. J. Stuermer, our assigned student liaison, calls the room to attention. We stand rigid and tense as Major Free slowly walks around the room and inspects each of us up and down. He stands at the center of the room and pauses.

Eyes dart around the room. Thirty-three dreams traveling on a single flight path. Sweat trickles down my back. What's he up to?

"Look to your left and right," he says. "One of you won't make it through UPT."

My breath catches.

Suddenly, my mind flashes back through the brutal years I just spent at the Air Force Academy—four long years of struggle, sacrifice, and hard work that got me into pilot training. And now this stranger is telling me I may not make it through?

A flood of resolve courses through my body, through my veins. I can barely stand still without vibrating.

The guy that doesn't make it—it won't be me.

I imagine my near future. I'll solo the Tweet. I'll earn those coveted silver wings, and my parents will pin them to my chest at UPT graduation. Then I'll strap into an F-16 jet fighter with thirty thousand pounds of thrust and lift off for greater heights.

I grin inside. This is no longer a training program for me—I'm now on a mission.

I commit to myself with a silent battle cry: I will do whatever it takes to fulfill my dreams. I will sweat; I will sacrifice; if necessary, I will bleed. I will advance the throttle of my life to full power and work my tail off.

I want those wings. I *will* push it up!

We all have dreams and aspirations that put a smile on our face and a surge of eagerness in our heart. What are yours? What launches you out of bed and into your day, ready to do whatever it takes to succeed?

Are you willing to fight for that success?

If you weren't, you wouldn't have bothered to pick up this book. Now that you have, don't put it down. It's the first step on a journey that will help you power through the barriers holding you back from reaching new heights in your career.

Trust me—if *I* can strap myself into the tiny cockpit of an F-16 for hours at a time, climb to thirty thousand feet over Iraq at Mach 2, and dodge oncoming missiles, then *you* can do anything.

You see, I was a claustrophobic fighter pilot with a fear of heights—not the best skill set for this line of work. And I couldn't tell a soul. Let's just say I was not your typical fighter pilot.

That's right. When I was a kid, I couldn't jump off a ten-foot-high diving board or even ride a roller coaster without being terrified. I was, for lack of a better word, a wimp. Then, three years into my eleven-year flying career, I nearly lost it while scuba diving in the Caribbean. My mask malfunctioned, and I inhaled a lungful of water. Panic ensued. I really thought I was going to die. Bursting up through the ocean surface with the one last breath in me, I told myself I would never scuba dive again. Not a pretty picture. The result? The latent claustrophobia that I thought I had overcome reared its ugly head, meaner and more fearsome than ever.

The next time I flew, I had a panic attack at twenty thousand feet. Suddenly dizzy and light-headed, I freaked out and swore my oxygen system was malfunctioning. I thought, *I have to get out of this cockpit . . . now!* The plane was perfect—it was all in my mind.

For the next eight years, I had to train myself to battle this fear. I could tell no one, or the Air Force would surely take my wings. It was my dirty little secret.

So picture me in the cockpit of an F-16 at twenty-five thousand feet, in the middle of a pitch-black sky, with a helmet and mask strapped to my face and barely enough room to shrug my shoulders. Some people call it claustrophobia. I call it a waking nightmare.

I know, fighter pilots are supposed to be steely-nerved superheroes with no fear, the confidence of a lion, and some very cool shades. Tom Cruise in real life, right? The thing is, that *Top Gun* stuff is mostly nonsense. Life isn't Hollywood, and neither is real combat. In a real fighter squadron, there are no mavericks and nobody cares who's good at volleyball. Up there, when the missiles are coming at you, the only things that count are your skills and ability to work as a team to get the job done—to make it happen. You don't even think for a second of flying solo.

In my time as an instructor pilot and an F-16 fighter pilot, I had severe anxiety, fear, and self-doubt flowing through my veins, and enough to spare—perhaps more than any other fighter pilot before me. No, I wasn't Tom Cruise or Val Kilmer, yet I flew sixty-five combat missions in enemy territory bristling with surface-to-air missiles, antiaircraft fire, and other deadly threats. It was an intense, monstrously difficult task that constantly pushed me to my limits and tested my commitment, but I did it. And I was never alone. I had help the entire way. And that, along with a few other key tools I'll be sharing in this book, is what made my success—and my very survival—possible.

I learned to push through my darkest secret fears, not only to earn my wings but also to live up to my duties and responsibilities as an Air Force officer—to protect and defend my country and my wingmen. My wingmen were there for the same reasons. And this is the embodiment of a team: people with different backgrounds, skills, and experiences unified under one agreement—to never think or act alone.

One team, one mission.

My mission in this book is to take you on the unlikely journey of a claustrophobic, acrophobic F-16 fighter pilot, revealing the lifesaving, career-making tools I picked up along the way—tools that will also enable you to break through whatever barriers are keeping you from soaring higher, faster, and freer. The process will teach you to trust and partner with yourself, the most important wingman you'll ever have. And, just as important, to surround yourself with a trusted team of partners who will make the journey with you. These are your wingmen, and the mutual trust you have with them will result in greater success, whatever the mission.

Although my journey involved high-speed aerial combat, the real essence of the battle to soar higher is no different from yours. We all have our personal demons to slay and obstacles to overcome. I took a path that was a little unconventional: climbing into a supersonic jet fighter to slay my phobias. The point is, if I could do that, *you* can power through *any* obstacle between you and your highest dreams.

FINDING THE MEANING IN YOUR MISSION

The journey can't begin until you find a mission in your work and life that is worth fighting for. I share this with you now because the rest of this book is meaningless until you commit yourself to a flight path you *believe* in. Not something a parent, partner, or well-meaning mentor thinks you should believe in—*you* have to own it, live it, breathe it. You then have to take absolute responsibility for your choices and, to complete the process, take determined action. Bottom line: before you can ever fly, you have to trust yourself and become passionate about your vision. After all, if you can't trust yourself—your wingman for life—who else is going to trust you?

Perhaps you want to be the number one sales producer in your company. Or maybe it's your dream to break free of the corporate world and be an entrepreneur. It doesn't matter whether you want to tackle a new leadership role at work, end hunger in Africa, or become the best parent you can be—first you have to know what your mission is.

Mine was born of a passion for excitement and challenge, along with a respect for my country that pushed me to break through the ceiling that was keeping me from reaching my highest potential. My mission to become a pilot required staring my phobias down and saying, "No. I will *not* let you define me. You can't drag me down!" Once I took this action and then surrounded myself with trusting men and women who were committed to breaking their own barriers and reaching new heights, my potential was unleashed and I was free to soar. The same will be true for you.

PUSHING IT UP

When I was stationed in South Korea with the 35th Fighter Squadron "Pantons," my wingmen and I had a secret handshake that demonstrated our commitment to each other and the mission. We would look each other in the eye and give the "hang loose" sign, which symbolized the eyes of the black panther, our squadron mascot. While thrusting this hand forward as if we were going to full-power-on throttle, we would roar out in a thunderous voice, "Push it up!" We all knew what it meant.

We were partners. We would think and act as one formation. We would protect each other and never leave another behind. We would be fully prepared and focused when it came time to fly. We were wingmen, *one team on one mission.* And in that, there was amazing freedom and confidence like nothing I had ever experienced. Come enemies, missiles, or unforeseen obstacles, I could succeed because *we* were succeeding.

I embraced the phrase "Push it up!" and carried it with me into my professional life. It has become a metaphor for taking fierce action for my personal mission and my team's mission. I encourage you to use it, too, because those three short words symbolize everything it takes to step onto—and stay on—the path to victory. It stands for maximum trust and maximum effort. It is the thrust that rockets you forward on the runway and into the air with confidence that you can fly, fight, and win.

You often hear people say that attitude determines altitude. This is only partly true. A more accurate formula is attitude *plus action* determines altitude.

I don't believe for a second that success is just about self-motivation. If that were all it took, all any of us would ever need is a little pep rally now and again and we'd soar to the stars. But after all the rah-rahs and the warm feelings wear off, it's ultimately about *action.* When you strap into your jet, you have to push up the throttle and then release the brakes to take off.

THE WORLD REWARDS PERFORMANCE, NOT PHILOSOPHY

"Push it up!" is about resolve combined with action. It means that you:

- Put forth consistent, maximum effort.
- Discipline yourself to take action every day.
- Stay focused (despite the missiles) until the mission is complete.
- Face adversity with courage.
- Know when to ask for help.

"Push it up!" is that one more sales call you make before you leave the office, and that extra hour of preparation before your meeting. It's the extra rep you do in the gym, and the investment you make in attending a personal development seminar. "Push it up!" is the things you do behind the scenes that your partners, coworkers, and customers never see. It is creating your future in your mind and then taking decisive action to make it happen.

"Push it up!" is resisting the temptation to ease up, get complacent, and pull back the throttle when you get tired, the going gets tough, or the fears and anxieties creep in. It's about being fully accountable for the results you get.

Let me reaffirm: Your customers, clients, and stockholders reward your *action*, not your attitude. They don't care about your attitude; they care about results. The only person who should be concerned with your attitude is you.

So here's the bottom line, my fellow wingmen. Jet fighters were not built to stay in the hangar and look impressive. They were meant to fly. And so are you.

My greatest desire is to help you fly. I want you to defeat the demons that have been holding you down and keeping you from taking off and reaching new heights in your career and your life. But first, you have to earn your wings.

Push it up!

WALDO'S WINGTIP

When engaging enemy forces in combat, the flight lead calls to his wingmen, "Commit! Commit!" This reaffirms to the rest of the formation that they are "going for it" and there is no turning back until the job is done.

True commitment only exists when it is aligned with action, which is based on disciplined preparation, laser focus, and, most of all, courage. This sort of courage says, "Even though I may get shot at, I will carry on."

Never take off on a mission unless you are 100 percent committed to victory. Before you commit to a product demonstration, a business meeting, or launching a new internal strategy, take time to reaffirm what it means to commit. Ask yourself (and your wingmen if they're with you) if you are truly willing to risk being shot at by the missiles of adversity, rejection, and change. Are you willing to risk failure? When the missiles are coming fast, will you push it up or pull it back? This is the true test of commitment.

When your partners and customers see how committed you are, they will become more loyal and will trust that you, rather than give up in the heat of battle, will push it up *for them.*

2

Chair Flying

The More You Sweat in Peace, the Less You Bleed in Battle

NOTHING CAN PREPARE you completely for a serious threat at thirty thousand feet. There is little room for error, and your first impulse is to panic. But your training has taught you to dismiss that feeling—your life depends on it. Your eyes and ears switch to full alert. Every sense is heightened. Your mental checklists are double- and triple-checked. Then training and instinct take over. Hopefully, you've done the thinking already, because now it's time to act.

In an F-16, hostile fire, bird strikes, engine failures, and bad weather threaten us every time we take flight. Each has the power to take us down. In business, the threats, though obviously different, are nonetheless serious. Sure, your life may not be on the line, but the life of the sale, your job, or your company may be. A sales objection, a missed deadline, task overload, or even the flu can take you down. How do you handle these hazards? Are you mission-ready, or do you go into a tailspin?

PREPARING FOR ADVERSITY DETERMINES THE OUTCOME

I used to think that attitude had a lot to do with how one responds to the missiles of business and life. But, the more time I spend in business, I am convinced that it's *how we prepare for adversity that determines the outcome*. In the world of the fighter pilot, the biggest factor that leads to success in the hostile and competitive world of combat is preparation, not attitude. Believe me, my wingmen and I didn't play motivational tapes in the mission planning room before combat! We prepared.

Preparation leads to power. And power means confidence and trust in our ability to handle any adversity in flight. We briefed the mission, studied the threat, formulated the tactics, delegated roles and responsibilities, and then most important, mentally rehearsed the mission. We contingency planned every emergency, missile launch, and possible threat. We call this "chair flying," and it played a critical role in our ability to win as a team of trusted partners when the stakes were high.

Everything is hypothetical until the battle begins. Anticipate the unexpected. From the moment tactics are planned, emergency procedures are outlined, communication requirements are set, and the target is plotted, until the mission is flown, there are no guarantees that things will go as planned. There is little margin for error, so preparation is absolutely critical to winning. The greater the preparation, the greater the ability to handle adversity, and the stronger the partnership that develops. For this reason, fighter pilots frequently assert, "The more you sweat in peace, the less you bleed in battle."

"FLEXIBILITY IS THE KEY TO POWER" (U.S. AIR FORCE SAYING)

To prepare for every scenario in battle, fighter pilots are taught to ask always, "What if . . . ?" *What if* the weather changes? *What if* one of us gets shot down or loses an engine? *What if* the tanker can't refuel us? We come up with a plan for every possible scenario and then execute those plans in our head—not while we're in flight but earlier, while sitting in a chair, strapped into a flight simulator, or during a mission briefing. We leave that briefing confident in our ability—and our wingmen's abilities—to adapt to change and to execute. In essence, we become more flexible.

Once again, it's not about walking to the jets motivated and with a positive attitude. We should already *be* motivated; otherwise, what are we doing in a flight suit? The only thing that ultimately matters is how we perform.

I first learned the habit of chair flying during pilot training at Williams Air Force Base in Arizona, when I was a young student struggling to learn all the maneuvers, radio calls, and emergency procedures with my classmates. The training was intense, stressful, and, at times, overwhelming. The instructors told us the best way for us to learn was to simulate flying while sitting down as if we were in the cockpit. If we had time, we would rehearse in the cockpit of an actual flight simulator. When at home, some students even used a plunger, stuck to the floor between their legs, as a mock control stick. The point was to rehearse the maneuvers in real time and carefully mimic each step or skill exactly as if we were flying four miles up at Mach 2.

Most of the work we did was in our minds, with subtle physical motions that supported the imagined event. Many pilots would close their eyes while chair flying and later reported feeling as though they were moving through the air. The mind has a way of preparing the body for everything, if we only allow it to.

You probably remember Capt. Chesley B. "Sully" Sullenberger and his crew on US Airways Flight 1549. On January 15, 2009, Sullenberger's Airbus A320 lost power in both engines after hitting a flock of birds on takeoff from LaGuardia Airport. Rapidly losing altitude and unable to reach an airport, Sullenberger took the only emergency runway available: the Hudson River. Cool and confident, Sully executed a plan. He and his crew knew exactly what to do, and his experience and skill, along with the teamwork of his wingmen, got that aircraft landed in the frigid waters. *All* 154 passengers survived.

Sully "chair flew" this mission dozens of times, and so did his crew. Their sweat and sacrifice *before* the emergency allowed them to execute with skill and confidence and save every passenger. Lives were transformed, and although the crew considered it all in a day's work, to everyone else they were heroes.

I'm sure there have been times at work when you felt as though you were landing a full plane on the Hudson with no engines. We've all been there. And the way you respond in a crisis can have profound lasting effects on your career and your organization. How many people have responded inappropriately to high-pressure circumstances and lost their job, reputation, partner, or investment? When the heat is on, the pressures of business can tempt us to make a rash decision that hurts the entire team. The sudden potential of a serious loss, or the opportunity to grab a quick buck, triggers an impulse decision, whether out of fear or self-interest or both, with devastating consequences that ripple outward, damaging or destroying lives and companies. It happens—sometimes to people not so different from you and me. We see it every day in the paper and on the news. At crunch time in business, a solid foundation of judgment and skill can mean the difference between success and catastrophe, and these qualities aren't acquired overnight.

WINGMEN NEVER "WING IT"

Lapses in judgment, inattention to detail, and just plain bad decisions are frequently the result of "winging it." We often use this phrase in a positive light, as if to suggest that we are sharp, innovative, and quick thinking, but the reality is that you should never *want* to wing it.

In short, winging it means you aren't prepared. In today's world, be it in a jet aircraft carrying a few hundred passengers, on a sales call, at a construction site, or in a hospital emergency room, there is no excuse for being unprepared. Captain Sully and his crew didn't wing it when they landed Flight 1549 in the Hudson. Rest assured, they didn't fly by the seat of their pants! They knew precisely what they were doing. And when at all possible, so should you.

The best way to prepare for any type of mission is simulation, and the ultimate simulator is the human mind. Use it! Mentally rehearse every mission.

When the first U.S. astronauts were training for the Mercury missions in the early 1960s, all they had in the way of a simulator was their brains, because no one had yet been to space. According to Dr. Charles Justiz, a NASA space shuttle instructor, the Mercury astronauts played out various emergencies and flight scenarios on grease boards, because spacecraft simulators were still too primitive to train on. They drilled each other on every procedure and contemplated every possible what-if and its outcome. By the time they flew their first mission, they had already played out most of the anticipated emergencies. This built their confidence, not just in the procedures but in each other.

THE COST OF PREPARATION

When fighter pilots go through training, they study hard and sweat a ton. Instead of watching TV, they hit the simulators and the books, work weekends, and essentially do whatever it takes to be the best pilots they can possibly be. They also prepare as a group, challenging and testing each other. Contrary to what you've seen in the movies, there has never been a "top gun" who spends more time playing volleyball and chasing women than preparing for the challenges of flight at Mach 2 and nine Gs. The more you sweat in peace . . .

The same truth applies in your career. There's a cost to winning. That's why I see WIN as an acronym for "work it now." What are you doing behind the scenes to win your next mission? How much are you "sweating in peace"?

The following chair-flying WingTips will help you prepare for your toughest missions and put you on the fast track to earning your business wings.

Ask "What If?" in Every Possible Scenario

The biggest part of every flight briefing is when pilots plan for contingencies and ask "what if?" What if the weather changes, the tanker isn't available to refuel, or a pilot has to land at an emergency runway? These realistic scenarios have already been flown by other pilots, and reams of data are available to use for planning. Therefore, when planning flights and chair-flying missions, gathering up-to-date intelligence and learning from the mistakes of others are crucial to successful execution.

Business books, magazines, and trade journals can be great intelligence sources for relevant training scenarios. Look for specific articles that outline descriptions and procedures for handling a particular business challenge. With today's powerful Web search engines, a minute or two of browsing is often all it takes to find helpful information. Then mentally rehearse how the information applies to your specific roles at work.

Coworkers or colleagues in your industry have already failed or succeeded at sales missions, marketing campaigns, and budget forecasts similar to yours. Learn from their experiences about what worked and what didn't, and then chair fly the best possible alternative actions. Always debrief after your chair flights and solicit feedback and suggestions from your entire team. Every situation or what-if requires its own specifically tailored response—no one action will work every time.

Always Fly with a Wingman

Rehearse scenarios with a wingman—preferably someone more experienced than you. There is a limit to how much you can learn on your own. A good wingman will give you mission-critical feedback, catch your errors, ask questions, and propose challenging scenarios to push you to grow in your skills and mental discipline. And practice especially with those wingmen on your team to whom you would most likely call out "Mayday!" when a missile launch comes.

Sales support, IT, finance, your office assistant, and even your spouse should participate in such sessions. And they do not all have to be face-to-face. Conference calls or Web meetings are great places to chair fly challenging scenarios at work, such as what to do when there are layoffs, budget cuts, missed sales projections, late shipments, bad weather, or even IT challenges such as a computer outage or Internet failure.

Break Down the Task into Manageable Chunks

At the beginning of Chapter 6, "Break Right!" I describe how I performed a complicated missile defense maneuver. If you look at all the steps as a whole, it can be quite overwhelming. But when chair flying, I would practice only one maneuver at a time until I got it perfect, and then string together the additional maneuvers. I would add more and more steps until I was able to perform the entire procedure by memory, with no mistakes.

When chair flying a new process, checklists are a very effective tool. They contain small, bite-size chunks of mission-critical information, along with cautions and warnings. Pilots strap them above their knee for quick and easy access in flight. Keep your checklists accessible when practicing your business missions. Consider all the steps involved in the sales process: greeting a customer or prospect, building rapport, asking questions about the prospect's business, providing product/service demonstrations, verbalizing next steps, setting up a follow-up meeting, asking for the sale, and so on. It's easy to get overwhelmed after the third or fourth step, but when you focus on mastering one step at a time, using a checklist to remind you of key items, it whittles down the stress and anxiety of trying to memorize the entire process.

Practice Under Pressure

Every unforeseen event brings on *some* anxiety and stress. That's normal. When a missile comes at you, you undergo what is known as a fight-or-flight response mechanism. Chair flying prepares you to fight to the best of your ability, knowing that no great achievement comes without a fierce battle.

Imagine an executive vice president taking the podium in front of 150 coworkers and going blank, or not knowing what to do when his PowerPoint presentation goes out during a crucial product demonstration for a big client.

While it's almost impossible to duplicate the exact environment of a given contingency, it is possible to simulate some of the pressures. And the truth is that it's more often the *pressure* of performing, not the act itself, that gets to us. For me, taking off was the toughest part of every combat mission. After I was airborne, 99 percent of the mission was already over, because I had done most of my work (and worrying) on the ground.

I challenge you to put some pressure on yourself by asking a wingman to challenge you with unplanned questions or what-if problems out of the blue. Or ask for a critique from a coworker or supervisor you trust. Consider practicing a new product presentation or sales pitch on a loyal customer whom you respect and with whom you already have a relationship. Implore the customer to be brutally honest with her feedback. You always learn the most from your customers, especially if they care about you and respect the relationship.

Finally, practice with distractions going on. Many people say it's best to study in a quiet room where there are no disturbances. But I say, not if disturbances can reach you in the real work arena. Think about it. In combat, distractions are always present. The cockpit can be quite noisy, with people bantering back and forth on the radios, and control panels lighting up. A pilot must still monitor the engines and fuel while handling an electrical problem. She must keep an eye on changing weather and make radio calls while cross-checking the position of her inexperienced wingman who is two miles away (and who may be struggling to keep her in sight). The pressure-cooker scenarios that come up in business demand your best judgment and skill amid various distractions. The more adept you are at operating under pressure and surrounded by distractions, the better you will be able to focus during real-time contingencies, with or without distractions.

After a stunning victory during the first Gulf War, Gen. Colin Powell, chairman of the Joint Chiefs of Staff—and, later, secretary of state—was asked for the secret to his overwhelming success. The military campaign was among the best planned and most precisely executed in modern warfare. Without a moment's hesitation, Powell replied, "There are no secrets to success. It is the result of preparation, hard work, and learning from failure."

Bingo! Success in battle is primarily a result of preparation—and at the core of that preparation is trust. Those soldiers who are prepared for all contingencies in battle are trustworthy. They are wingmen. They are the ones you want in your formation when the missiles come.

Who, then, are *your* allies—your coalition? Can you count on them to be well prepared? Can they count on you for the same? Fighter pilots don't go into battle expecting to lose. We are prepared—and expect—to be victorious. So should you.

As a general rule, one hour of flight time means four hours of planning. That may look like a disproportionate investment, but it pays handsome dividends. Are you doing the work before you strap into your jet to fly? What goes on behind the scenes before your performance on the job? This is the stuff that your coworkers, managers, and customers don't see. It's the extra hours polishing up a PowerPoint presentation for a key meeting and fielding every tough question you can come up with. It's the double- and triple-checking of the projectors and sound systems to make sure your presentation goes off without a hitch. It's the additional research into your customer's portfolio and press releases that can give you an advantage and set you apart from your competitors. Success is never an accident, and making it look easy takes a lot of hard work.

The best place to prepare is on the job. Develop a contingency plan with a wingman and base it on a realistic scenario. Start with small challenges and raise the stakes from there. Ask your wingmen to monitor your performance and give feedback. Be willing to make mistakes, and keep a positive attitude. Practice until the actions flow effortlessly. You may be astonished at how effective this strategy is.

Before your next sales call or business presentation, do fifteen minutes of focused chair flying. I guarantee you and your wingmen will notice a major difference in your confidence and performance.

And Finally, Focus

Thrust is your *effort*; vector is your *direction*. Here's a key: don't be all *thrust* and no *vector*. People who are all thrust fly by the seat of their pants. They're fired up and excited to do battle, but they have no real plan or even a target to hit. They are easily blown off course by the winds of change, challenge, and adversity.

One of my favorite quotes is "Beware of distractions disguised as opportunities." People who are all thrust are often easily distracted by what appear to be opportunities. They're cruising along just fine until the phone rings, their e-mail indicator chimes, or a friend drops by the office. Something small throws them off course, and all that productive momentum flies off on a tangent. Getting such people airborne and on target again requires a ton of thrust. They take off at full speed in any old direction and end up taking twice the time to complete their tasks, if they complete them at all. They make horrible wingmen. Real wingmen are "on time, on target" and stay focused on the task at hand.

You may be wondering about multitasking. Is it OK to multitask when the heat is on? Well, it used to be considered a badge of honor to call oneself a multitasker. The impression was that this jack-of-all-trades was indispensable and infinitely resourceful. But recent studies have concluded that multitasking is really a model of inefficiency. It diverts focus from mission-critical areas and can leave many tasks ineptly or incompletely done.

For a fighter pilot, multitasking is unavoidable and quite important, but it can get you killed if not applied correctly. There is a time to blow off all non-mission-critical items and focus solely on the task at hand. If you try to do too much, you'll crash and burn. This is why it's so important to fly with wingmen—they can accomplish various supporting tasks as you tackle the high-priority target. In your professional life, excessive multitasking can cripple your performance and even shoot down your career. Focus is crucial to success, whether you're in a cockpit, a cubicle, or a boardroom.

A regular dose of intensive, real-world chair flying will help you practice focusing. By rehearsing your responses to the bad weather and hostile fire that are a necessary part of business, you'll be on your way to earning your wings. You'll be mission ready no matter what circumstances come your way—and your wingmen will be enthusiastic partners.

WALDO'S WINGTIP

How do you prepare for your business missions?

- Are you chair flying your sales calls to ensure success?
- Do you practice different delivery styles and opening/ closing statements?
- Do you have planned answers to standard sales objections?
- Are you gathering intelligence on your prospect and your competitors?
- Do you envision success in your mind *before* executing your new strategy?

Chair flying builds confidence as it reduces your fear of failure and gives you more courage to take risks. So stop *flying by the seat of your pants* and start *chair flying*. Not only will your clients, coworkers, and managers grow to trust you, but you'll also build more trust in the most important wingman in your life: you.

3

Check Six

Wingmen: They Have Your Back, and You Have Theirs

ON JANUARY 19, 1991, the president's order came, and Operation Desert Shield suddenly became Operation Desert Storm. The skies over Baghdad lit up with antiaircraft artillery, and coalition forces launched missiles from sea and air against the city's highest-value targets. The "mother of all battles" had begun.

Some twenty thousand feet overhead, Package Q, the single largest strike mission of the war and likely the single largest F-16 strike package ever flown into combat, was in flight.

During one particularly harrowing moment, Maj. Emmett "ET" Tullia was caught in an intense game of cat and mouse with ground-based missile systems. He was the mouse.

Surface-to-air missiles (SAMs) locked on to ET's jet, and the pilot needed every ounce of training and instinct he possessed.

"Stroke Three, c'mon, break right! Break right!" blared the frantic voice of the flight lead.

"SAM launch!" yelled another.

"Stroke Three, go southeast . . . *now*!"

"Break right! Break right! Stroke Three, break right!"

"OK, Stroke Three is OK. Wait . . . another SAM lock! Another SAM lock!"

Silence.

The frenzied voices in ET's headset caused him to climb, dip, roll, and push his F-16 to the limit of its capacity.

No less than six SAMs were launched at ET that evening, and any one of them could have ended his life in an eye blink.

But ET wasn't flying solo. His wingmen were monitoring his every move as well as the enemy's—they had his back.

They were checking his six.

Check six is fighter pilot terminology for watching your teammate's back. It refers to the six o'clock position, where the jet is most vulnerable. It's the pilot's blind spot.

When a fighter pilot is strapped into the tiny cockpit of an F-16, he can barely move. Clamped into a mask and helmet, with a lap belt cinched across his waist, and a shoulder harness lashing him to the seat back, he can wiggle side to side only three or four inches. This lack of mobility and the back end of the jet make it all but impossible to see your own six o'clock.

Let's do a quick exercise. Without cheating (remember, you have only a few inches to move), try to turn your head and body enough to look directly behind you at your six o'clock. Just about impossible, right? Now imagine someone is seated five to ten feet to your right, and look over there. I bet it's a lot easier to see your wingman's six o'clock than to see your own!

But your wingman can check your six. The following diagram shows the sight line of two fighter pilots in combat formation. We literally watch each other's back for all threats.

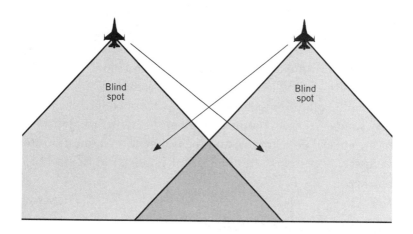

A threat normally comes from where we can't see it. That's what makes it such a threat: we don't know it's there. Checking each other's six means we're constantly watching our wingmen's most vulnerable spot for threats to their safety and to the mission. Missiles and enemy aircraft always try to attack from the rear. Not only that, it's impossible for a pilot to see if he's on fire, leaking fuel, or has some structural damage. He needs a wingman to observe these threats, too. For this reason, wingmen can never doubt each other's intentions. We must act on the advice of our wingmen and trust that when we hear "Break right!" it's for a good reason.

Timing can be a critical factor. You don't always have the luxury of checking and double-checking your wingman's judgment when the missiles are locked and launched. In the fighter pilot world we have a saying: "Speed is life." If you don't respond to a threat immediately, you're dead. How often does this hold true in business?

Today, your speed to market your product, meet customer demands, adapt to changing technology, and correct a negative course are critical to survival, let alone success. If your boss, the market, or your customer says, "Break right," you'd better listen. Respond too slowly, and your career, your sale, or even your company is vulnerable to a fatal blow. The object lessons are everywhere: the rapid and complete transformation of the photo industry by the digital transition, the shifting sands of the computer industry owing to constant technological innovations, and the floundering domestic auto industry all demonstrate the critical importance of speed to market.

THE THREE KEY COMPONENTS OF CHECKING SIX

Capt. Chris Rose of the District of Columbia Air National Guard was returning to Andrews Air Force Base from a training mission June 27, 1996, when his F-16C Fighting Falcon had a flameout at thirteen thousand feet. He was forced to land the fighter at Elizabeth City Air Station in North Carolina, fifteen miles from the point of engine failure. His fellow fighter pilots worked as a team to get him on the ground safely.

With no engine and gliding on backup power, he had his team of wingmen with him the whole way—two F-16s above and one, piloted by Lt. Col. Vince Shiban, flying in chase formation behind him. Shiban alerted the tower about the emergency. The only thing Rose had to do was glide the plane in and hope its electrical backup system worked. Not as easy as it sounds.

Once he jettisoned his wing tanks to reduce weight and drag, Rose then had a problem with the landing gear. After engaging the emergency gear-extension system, he finally got the gear down and locked.

His wingmen did all the communicating with the tower so that Rose could stay focused and literally glide the plane in to land. On final approach, Shiban made a call to the tower: "Tower, confirm he is cleared to land. *He is an emergency.* He is engine-out, his gear is down, he's on short final!" Tower acknowledged his clearance.

"You're doing good. *You got three green; you look good!*" Shiban called out to Rose, confirming that his gear was down and locked.

That problem solved, Rose still had to land on a runway that was a thousand feet shorter than the recommended length for a flameout landing. He landed two thousand feet down its length, then had to stop very carefully because he was using a limited emergency braking system. He came to a halt a mere thousand feet from the end.[1]

Captain Rose breathed normally and sounded calm, cool, and relaxed during the entire emergency.

This truly is a perfect example of training and mutual support in the fighter pilots' world. The pilot's success (and survival) can be attributed to three things:

1. **Effective communication.** Obviously, Captain Rose was under intense pressure. He had only one shot at landing that aircraft. And if he hadn't managed to make the runway, he would have had to bail out of the jet. Not only are low-

---

1. National Guard Association of the United States, "Air Guard Fighter Pilot Receives Air Force's Koren Kolligian Trophy," *National Guard*, May 1997, http://findarticles.com/p/articles/mi_qa3731/is_199705/ai_n8771125.

altitude ejections very unsafe, but the unpiloted jet could crash into a school, a home, a hospital, or a shopping mall. His wingmen served as a chase ship, talked him down, and checked his six, ensuring that his gear was down so that he could stay focused on the most critical task at hand: landing that jet. Lieutenant Colonel Shiban didn't *need* to say, "You look good." But he had the situational awareness to realize that in the heat of this emergency, giving his wingman some encouragement was probably a good thing to do. With his reassuring and comforting positive voice, Shiban was a "comrade of courage." Rose knew that Shiban and the others had his back and that everything was OK.

Remember, Shiban also communicated with another unsung hero and key wingman, the tower controller, to make sure that Rose was cleared to land and that no other aircraft were on the runway.

In the business world, we all experience engine failures at times and need to land our jets under extremely adverse conditions. No one is immune—layoffs, budget cuts, extended work hours, the relentless pressure to perform, constantly changing technology, or a family emergency can trigger an engine flameout at any time. If and when it happens, having a wingman to check in with us and back us up can make all the difference. Sometimes all it takes is a "check-in" on the radio and perhaps a little encouragement to help us to land. At other times, we may need a wingman to take over certain responsibilities so we can focus on the challenge at hand. This is the key to partnering at work.

As leaders on and off the job, we need to keep our visual cross-check and communication consistent and not forget about those who lock themselves in the office and become "lost" at work. Sure, they may be doing a great, vitally important job, but if no one is checking in with them or has an active interest in them as a person, who's going to know if they have a flameout?

It isn't the worker who is well covered and accountable—the disciplined and focused worker with wingmen watching his back—who blunders royally or just falls apart one day. It's the worker who keeps to himself—the one trying to fly solo. If someone isn't checking a worker's six, then guess what? That worker checks out! Employees who check out become unmotivated, complacent, and careless. Never feeling invested in the company's mission, they do the minimum, and everyone suffers.

But when their peers communicate with them and they feel appreciated and part of the team, workers get sparked with motivation to contribute to the mission. They go the extra mile, check their paperwork a little more carefully, and treat the customer with more respect. And everyone wins.

As a wingman and partner at work, you should communicate and check six by asking, counseling, encouraging, and suggesting. Do this with your peers and partners, not just with your subordinates and your boss. Not only will this build trust and lay the foundation for more effective partnerships, it will also raise your confidence level as a leader. Your stress level will drop, and you'll breathe easier knowing someone is there on your wing to help you land should an emergency arise.

2. **Honest feedback.** Checking six also means monitoring your wingmen for changes in their behavior that threaten their success. This is where brutal honesty comes into play. No one wants to hear negative feedback on his or her performance, but feedback is critical to sustained success. That

shoe fits the other foot, too—you have to be able to put aside your ego and be open to feedback. It's vitally important that you have the courage to give and receive feedback, especially when it's something you or your wingman may not want to hear.

As a trusted wingman, you have to be willing to *give and receive* those "break right" calls, just as Major Tullia did when dodging those SAMs over Iraq. Lieutenant Colonel Shiban also gave feedback vital to the success of the mission in his communications with Captain Rose and the tower controller. He explained the entire situation and made sure expectations were clear. He even made sure to tell Captain Rose to "get the aircraft stopped." Did Rose need to hear that? Probably not. Of course he knew that he needed to stop the jet! But Shiban knew that in stressful situations, even the most basic tasks can be overlooked or botched, sometimes out of sheer nervousness.

Sometimes when handling an emergency or engaging a target, fighter pilots get "task saturated." Task saturation means that one is so fixated or engrossed in the task at hand that she cannot cross-check other mission-critical items or communicate with her wingmen. As a result, she may not see a possible missile or other factor that can affect her jet or the mission. In a heartbeat, she turns from a supporting wingman to a solo flier. Moreover, she may not think she has a problem until the wingmen who are checking her six give her feedback.

Good wingmen will keep you aware of your surroundings, build your situational awareness (SA), and make sure you don't get shot down. They'll let you know you're burning the candle at both ends or stressed out beyond your limits. They'll make sure you stay in contact with your customers and loved ones. They will also let you know when you're messing up. And, most important, they will warn you when you don't have the judgment to make good decisions on your own.

In the fighter pilot debrief, it is common practice to remove our name tags and rank markings to create an open, nonretributive environment. The senior ranking officer is treated the same as a raw young wingman. All give feedback, admit errors, and call out each other's mistakes. This improves training and even saves lives, as egos are put aside for the sake of the mission. This is a great practice to model in business.

3. **Mutual support.** I'm guessing you have picked up by now that you must embody the same qualities you expect of your wingmen. As the wingmen in your life are watching your back, you must watch theirs. In fact, the more present and helpful you are in their service, the more on the spot they will be for you.

Mutual support is critical for "checking six" to work, because its effectiveness depends on a two-way commitment. You never know when the engine failure or the missiles will come—and neither do your wingmen. The only way to be sure someone has your back at all times is when both parties know, without a shadow of doubt, that their wingman is there for them.

YOU DON'T NEED A FLIGHT SUIT TO BE A WINGMAN

In a fighter squadron, the ones wearing flight suits and flying the jets aren't the only wingmen. We have intelligence personnel briefing us about the various threats, the weather staff updating us on changing weather conditions, the maintenance crew keeping the planes airworthy, and the tanker crews refueling us in the air. Many times, these wingmen are behind the scenes, providing support to the frontline fighter pilots. If they don't do their job correctly, we can't do ours. We're only as strong as our weakest link.

This "one team, one mission" mentality is what inspires a check-six culture across the entire organization. Since no one person can be aware of all the obstacles and dangers in the environment, every wingman provides a unique perspective that can build awareness and up the team's odds for success. By creating trusting relationships with all the wingmen in your unit, *you increase commitment, because everyone has a stake in the outcome.* All partners become aligned with the mission and will go the extra mile to make sure it gets accomplished.

In a wingman culture, a wingman who checks six can see the big picture and recognize changes in another wingman's behavior. The wingman can see how the stress in a person's life can alter their behavior, and may be able to help that person. A check-six environment is one in which a wingman will always come to the aid of another and never leave him behind.

Just like Lieutenant Colonel Shiban, a wingman will serve as a chase ship and guide her buddy to a landing or to a resource where he can get help. This isn't just about encouraging. It's about taking action and making sure your wingman is taken care of.

CREATING A CHECK-SIX ENVIRONMENT

When communication, feedback, and mutual support don't exist, people begin to distrust each other. No one collaborates, fear arises, and the team lacks synergy. Inevitably, overall performance suffers. But when people trust, miracles in productivity and morale can happen. In fast-paced, high-risk, performance-demanding environments like the world of business, tight and trustworthy coordination is critical because:

- Human beings make mistakes.
- We each have a limited perspective.
- We operate in stressful environments that lead to tunnel vision and task saturation.
- Most professionals undervalue communication and teamwork.
- Faulty communication can kill a mission as well as a relationship.
- Errors increase when there is no definable set of teamwork standards and skills.

An effective check-six environment frees up communication and removes barriers to growth so that *all members of the team feel empowered to speak up and ask questions.* Most important, it creates a context in which feedback and objective criticism are received more openly and less defensively. Team members become more engaged in processes and service, while leaders benefit from the improved flow of vital information up and down the chain of command.

A check-six environment also builds team confidence. It is the experienced manager who goes on a big sales call with the younger salesperson to provide support; it is the safety spotter on a highway construction zone; and it is the officer who pulls his squad car behind a fellow officer's during a routine traffic stop. It is the CEO who leaves his office empty every afternoon to spend quality time on the floor and in the warehouse with his workers. Measures such as these promote team culture and effectiveness like nothing else.

USE YOUR CHASE SHIP FOR BATTLE DAMAGE ASSESSMENT

After every training and combat mission, fighter pilots line up as "two-ships" and methodically maneuver under and behind each other's aircraft to observe any structural damage, leaks, bird strikes, and so on that may have gone unnoticed during the mission. We call this a "battle damage check" and put our trust in our wingmen to look over every detail to make sure the jet is perfect before we head back home. If there is a problem, an emergency is declared, and a chase ship is assigned to the problem aircraft. No wingman is ever left to handle a problem on his own. Just as Lieutenant Colonel Shiban helped Captain Rose land safely, we, too, need to be wingmen to each other and be ready to perform chase-ship duties on short notice.

Imagine how such a practice could affect your work life.

In today's challenging economy, with the "missiles" of layoffs, budget cuts, high unemployment, diminishing investments, foreclosures, and high-pressure work environments, sooner or later we're all going to get shot at, take some hits, and receive some battle damage. The key is, let's not get shot down. And that also means not letting our wingmen get shot down.

We can do this by checking our wingmen's six and being a chase ship when we see one of them struggling. We can lend our wings to our partners and peers at home and at work. We can provide as much mutual support, encouragement, and feedback as possible and call out "Break right!" when necessary. We can make sure they have "three green" and are cleared to land.

Sure, emergencies are never fun. But if we can get back on the ground safely and debrief, then we can fly another mission with greater confidence and reach new heights.

In the end, checking six is about trusting others to see what you can't see, and it's also about putting in the effort to see what your wingmen can't see. Sure, it takes work and discipline to accomplish, but it's nothing less than the foundation for all partnerships.

Nobody likes to hear they have blind spots—areas of vulnerability—but our blind spots are there whether or not we're aware of them. By having an extra pair of eyes checking our six, we stay protected from the ever-increasing threats and are more able to focus on hitting the target. Checking six will help us all return to base as one unified team, ready to fly again. And at the end of the day, this is what really matters.

WALDO'S WINGTIPS

Here are four more WingTips for creating a check-six culture in your organization:

- Start by asking others for authentic feedback on your performance. Ask them to sit in on a sales call or meeting that you're leading. Ask for one-on-one honest feedback on their view of you and your performance. Yes, your ego might get dinged, but you'll come out of it a better, stronger leader.
- If you are a formal leader or manager, openly reward those who demonstrate values of mutual support by creating a "Wingman of the Quarter" award. It can set

a positive tone in your organization and motivate people to check each other's six.

- Be willing to say, "I don't know," or "I messed up." Your transparency will attract others to you and create the type of environment where people won't be afraid to make mistakes. They will also be more likely to check your six as well.

- Keep your radar sweeping for a wingman, coworker, or peer who may be experiencing a challenging time in her life. Don't let her get isolated. Lend her a wing, be supportive, and find her some help if necessary. Remember, this doesn't have to be somebody you have a formal relationship with.

4

Over-G

Integrity First: A Wingman's #1 Core Value

INSTRUCTOR PILOTS RARELY get to fly solo, but this was my lucky day. With no student to monitor and no painfully long debrief to deliver, I was going to make the most of it. Today it was just me, my Cessna T-37B "Tweet" twin-engine jet trainer, and the wide-open skies above Enid, Oklahoma.

I finished my aerobatics and stall maneuvers in the military operating area (MOA) and returned to the traffic pattern at Vance Air Force Base, where I had just enough fuel left to practice a few touch-and-gos at the base. The T-37 was a very maneuverable and rugged trainer, built to withstand punishment from inexperienced and aggressive student pilots. Its structural G limit was 6.67 Gs—the maximum strain the airframe could endure before possible damage occurred. As I turned crosswind and climbed to a thousand feet above the ground, a thought crossed my mind: why not see how close I could come to pulling 6.67 Gs? It's a question that changed the trajectory of my career.

Turning downwind, I pushed up the throttles to full power and reached 220 knots of airspeed (about 250 miles per hour). I banked the jet ninety degrees to the right and pulled back on the stick for several seconds, feeling the G force compress me into my ejection seat. I looked down: 4.9 Gs—weak!

Disappointed in myself, I pushed up the throttles and waited for the jet to accelerate once again. Bank and pull: 5.6 Gs. Still not satisfied, I knew I could get it closer to 6.67 than that.

One more try, only this time I hit a little bit of low-altitude turbulence, and it jostled my hand. I did what pilots call "pulsing the stick" and overcorrected by yanking back on the control stick a little too hard. I looked down at the G meter: 7 Gs.

For a split second, I felt a sense of victory. Yes! I had taken the jet to its limits. I won!

But then I had what they refer to in psychoanalysis as "a moment of clarity." I knew I had over-G'd the jet and, technically, could have caused structural damage. According to flying regulations, I was supposed to declare an emergency and land the jet immediately. But my first instinct was to reach over and punch off the G meter (like setting an odometer back to zero). After all, I had seen other, more experienced pilots do it before. If they did it, why couldn't I? And besides, the T-37 was tough as nails. What was .33 extra Gs going to do to it?

So here I was, flying around as a cocky young captain with a difficult choice to make: zero out the G meter, land the jet, and act as if nothing had happened, or admit my mistake on the radio by declaring an emergency, land the potentially damaged jet, and accept the consequences. My commander would have my head, and my reputation in the squadron would be tarnished.

I cringed as I pondered what my wingmen at Vance would think of me. *Waldo, the slacker. Waldo, the hotdogger. What a punk. I don't want to fly with that guy.*

And then I thought to myself, what if my twin brother were to fly that jet tomorrow and the wing fell off? What if my best friend in the squadron got into a spin he couldn't recover from and had to bail out? Would the seat eject properly? Or were the ejection rails bent just enough to cause a malfunction? What if I caused a hairline crack in the airframe, invisible to the eye, that would cause the plane to break apart in flight? My choice became instantly clear. But trust me, that didn't mean it was easy to act on.

I declared the emergency.

"State nature of emergency," the tower controller replied.

"Uh, over-G," I replied with a slight pause. I had a feeling they knew I had messed around in the jet.

I nervously pondered my demise as I landed and slowly taxied back to the parking area. I debriefed the maintenance crew and operations officer and was directed to the office of my squadron commander, where I had a very intimate "come to Jesus" meeting (a rather big deal for a Jewish guy!).

Let's just say Lieutenant Colonel Stallworth wasn't pleased.

My actions were irresponsible and showed a serious lack of discipline. I had also put myself and others in an unsafe situation. Not only was I severely reprimanded, I was grounded from flying for two weeks, the length of time the jet would be out of commission. I also had to present a briefing to the squadron on the twenty-five-thousand-dollar mainte-nance procedure necessary to inspect the jet for structural damage. Fortunately, the inspection revealed no damage to the aircraft. Still, I had cost my wingmen valuable training time and put a serious ding in my reputation. The job promotion I wanted would probably never happen.

Take a few minutes and think back to a situation where your integrity was tested. Have you ever had to choose between damaging your career by admitting a mistake or protecting your career by keeping quiet? The right choice matters more than you might think.

There are several lessons that we can draw from my experience.

- **Your integrity affects everyone.** Had I failed to turn myself in and admit my mistake, a major accident could have resulted—perhaps even killing one of my wingmen. Sure, the chances were minimal. But was it a risk I was willing to accept? There's always more at stake than your reputation, and when I really thought about this, my choice became clear. Your actions have consequences that reach far outside your cockpit, affecting others, and those effects may not come about until years later. This is a critical concept to grasp if you are to be a trusted wingman. And you must surround yourself with people who also understand this. Without integrity, there can be no trust. Partnerships erode, and mission-readiness falters.

- **Integrity should not be a choice.** Integrity should be instinctive. You should do the right thing, even when no one is watching. It's not something that begins and ends at work—integrity is twenty-four hours a day or it is nothing. Fighter pilots are expected to maintain the highest standards of integrity in everything they do—a vitally important expectation considering the dangerous nature of our work. If I can't trust you to do the right thing at home or in the squadron, how far can I trust you in combat, when the stakes are highest? A true wingman does what is right and lets the sticks fall where they may.

• **Rank has its responsibilities as well as its privileges.** As an officer in the Air Force, I had (and still have) a responsibility to comply with the flying regulations and standards of my squadron. It's called being a professional. And in the military, we have a higher calling, with more exacting standards, because lives are on the line. As a member of your company, you, too, must comply with its regulations and standards of behavior, whether or not you agree with them. If you can't abide by those rules you have no business being in that position and drawing that paycheck. There's a bigger picture, a greater ecology, than your personal niche in the organization, and the regulations and standards are in place to protect that greater good. While selfish or wrongheaded leaders can at times create unproductive, even detrimental, regulations, there is always a way to address the problem with integrity rather than with maverick behavior.

CUTTING CORNERS DOESN'T SQUARE UP

At the U.S. Air Force Academy, one of the first things we learned as fourth-class cadets (freshmen) was the honor code: "We will not lie, steal, or cheat, nor tolerate among us anyone who does." We also were taught the core values of the Air Force, starting with "integrity first." The code and our core values were drilled into us from day one of basic training, laying the foundation for all our behavior at the academy and in our careers.

As we all can attest, sometimes the rules don't make sense. We had a few of those at the academy. I remember an incident that happened when I was an eighteen-year-old fourth-class cadet. The regulations required that we walk at attention at all times when not in our room. Stiff, braced walk, chin in, arms straight. Shoulders back and down. Square every corner. This and many other rules at the academy seemed petty, but they were the rules and we were expected to follow them.

After finishing class early one day, I returned to what appeared to be an empty dorm. As I approached my room and prepared to make a rigid and disciplined left face, I decided to let my arms flail and bolt right into my room. Who would see me? I closed the door and giggled like a little kid who has gotten away with something.

In less than ten seconds, a pounding on my door made me jump. It was Cadet Third Class David W. Smith, roommate of Cadet Will Reese, a hardcore master trainer. You did not want to get on either one's bad side. "Nice job, Cadet Waldman. You think the rules don't apply when no one is watching? Why don't you join Cadet Reese and me for lunch tomorrow?"

I was doomed.

For the next month, my life was miserable. They hammered me every day with incessant uniform inspections, five extra "current events" (from the local news) per day to memorize, and a slew of other exercises in attitude adjustment. Not only was it a pain, it was humiliating. But I got the point. Who wants to be a wingman (especially in combat) with someone they can't trust to do the right thing when no one is watching? And while my squaring corners in an empty dormitory hall really had no effect on others, I learned a valuable lesson: integrity isn't a game that one plays at.

Gen. George S. Patton famously said, "You are *always* on parade." How true. A trustworthy wingman has integrity even when no one is looking.

Everyone knew the consequences of noncompliance at the academy, but still we broke some of the rules. Cadets cheated and lied and did the things that most eighteen- to twenty-two-year-old kids do. Disciplinary action ranged from demerits to marching tours to sitting in solitary confinement. The point sank in: follow regulations and abide by the honor code, or suffer the consequences.

The academy taught me that my actions and integrity (or lack thereof) had consequences, that what I did or didn't do affected others. Of course, occasional lapses in integrity are expected from teenagers and young adults, but at thirty, forty, fifty years old? Look at the tally of major companies that have collapsed over the past ten years. How many examples do we need before we get the picture?

Sure, there's a difference between the training world of the Air Force Academy and the business world, but the consequences of flouting the rules can be just as dire. No wingmen were watching the so-called leaders of failed corporate highflyers such as Enron or WorldCom. There was no honor code except the one they devised to help themselves. Accountability was nonexistent. The results were lost careers, jail, depleted life savings, and irreparably broken families—and, yes, even lost lives. Many sad tales begin with someone ignoring one rule one time. But after setting even one foot on that slippery slope, they found it increasingly difficult to get off without sliding all the way down.

SMALL CRACKS LEAD TO BIG CRACKS

There's another reason fighter pilots are held to such high standards of integrity, especially where things like the G meter are concerned. On the body of a fighter jet, a hairline crack less than an inch long can lead to fatal consequences. Before the advances of modern engineering, many combat jets went down in battle not from enemy fire but because the tiniest of cracks went undetected. At Mach speeds, the pressure on the wings is tremendous, and a tiny crack, invisible to the human eye, can quickly run the width of the wing under the right conditions.

In November 2007, an Air Force F-15C Eagle jet fighter crashed because of a defective beam on its airframe. The pilot was barely able to eject from the plane as it literally broke apart beneath him. Investigators later discovered a crack in the beam near the fuselage that had grown over time and had previously gone undetected during maintenance inspections.

Will you make mistakes in your career? Yes. Most will be minor ones—small cracks in your wing. Perhaps they will go unnoticed. You will also likely bear witness to others making mistakes. The real question is, will you have the courage to come clean with your cracks and confront others about theirs? Or will you be more concerned with not ruffling feathers or rocking the boat? Often, if *you* don't take the right action, no one will. What example are you setting for your wingmen? The cracks will only grow with time.

The best way to create an environment where your wingmen will live and work with integrity is by having the courage to admit your own mistakes. Leadership expert John C. Maxwell calls this "the law of magnetism," explaining, "Who you are is who you attract."[1]

In the Air Force, we call the ability to admit mistakes "exposing your chest to daggers." For example, no mission we fly is ever complete until we go through a debrief. The

1. John Maxwell, *The 21 Irrefutable Laws of Leadership* (Nashville: Thomas Nelson, 1999).

debrief is where true learning occurs. We review everything about the mission and look for areas to improve our mission effectiveness. During the debrief, the flight lead who is in charge of the mission starts off by admitting his or her mistakes or blunders in front of the entire team. This paves the way for others to admit theirs. If a young wingman brand-new to the squadron makes a mistake (or witnesses a safety violation from a senior wingman), he will feel more willing to admit his mistake, give honest feedback, or call out "break right." If we are truly committed to excellence, we need to put our egos aside and hear the truth. When the stakes are high, rank has no place, in the briefing room or in business.

Your personal integrity is the foundation of the professional culture you build around yourself. It is the core of your inner wingman. And having the integrity to admit your mistakes—despite the possible hit to your reputation—sends a clear message: you expect nothing less from those around you.

When faced with a difficult decision, you cannot go wrong asking yourself these four questions:

- **What does your gut say?** You know deep down whether it feels right.
- **How will it affect others?** Think of how your actions (or inaction) will affect your wingmen in both the near and long term.
- **What will the consequences be if I don't "fess up" and am found out?** Keep the cleanup under your control as much as possible. You can't avoid all consequences, but you can minimize them. Remember, even a small mess, if left alone, eventually starts to stink up the entire house. Clean up your messes quickly.

- **How can I reestablish trust?** Start by saying (publicly if possible) two magic words that are rarely heard today: "I'm sorry." Then stop beating yourself up over the infraction and get about the work of repairing trust.

In 1994, during a weekend air show in Washington State, a perfectly operational B-52 military aircraft crashed in a horrifying blaze. The pilot had exceeded the maximum bank angle for the B-52 at low altitude, which caused the plane to stall. The pilot and three crew members were killed and the community and hundreds of lives were devastated. The pilot was a maverick who repeatedly violated flying regulations but was never grounded for his mistakes. Many knew of these breaches but simply turned a blind eye, and those who spoke up got no support from the wing commander, whom the pilot was friendly with. The commander failed to ground him for his poor airmanship, and this lack of leadership played just as big a role as the pilot's hotdogger mentality in the tragedy. As commander, he should have held the pilot accountable to Air Force standards. Instead, he mirrored the pilot's lack of integrity. By ignoring smaller consequences, the commander let them grow to catastrophic proportions.

I can't emphasize this enough: your level of integrity has huge implications. Your actions may not cost the lives of your crew, but you might destroy your reputation, your department, your company, your partnerships, or even your family. As a leader, you must also be willing to risk losing the relationship with someone who lacks integrity for the benefit of your organization. If the wing commander had disciplined and grounded the maverick B-52 pilot whom he was friendly with and put the needs of his troops first, four lives may have been saved.

It isn't that hard to get away with tax evasion, manipulating stock prices, cooking the books, cheating on your spouse, or a whole litany of other dishonorable practices—at least for a while. No one may know right away, but sooner or later the truth will come out. All decisions lacking integrity come down to some combination of arrogance, selfishness, and fear. People are generally afraid of consequences and lack the courage to do the right thing. Their image is more important than their integrity, and in the end, they have neither. It is much harder—and more perilous—to keep up a false image than to reveal a damaged but honest one.

Remember, integrity isn't just about being honest—it's also about being able to admit when you haven't been. It's about admitting when you mess up and accepting the consequences. So, what will you do the next time you're faced with a tough choice about integrity?

In business, you may be off course, miss a crucial deadline, get the pricing wrong on an order, or badly miss a budget projection. It can take a day or two to get back on course—certainly not a desirable option. But consider the alternative: if you delay longer than you should, it may take you a month or two months, even years, to get back on course. It may cost you your job or the company the account. As hard as it may seem, a good wingman will value a speedy confession and will even help you get back on track.

So if you want your wingmen to live with integrity, have the courage to admit *your* mistakes and "over-Gs." When you do what you say you're going to do, and expect nothing less of others, performance improves. This is the foundation for creating a culture of courage. Integrity is contagious, and it has to start from the top down. Moreover, when you shift the focus off yourself and onto how your actions affect your mission, coworkers, customers, partners, and family, you become a more trusted wingman.

Courage builds character. It's the foundation of integrity. It gives you the thrust to make the correct choices and do what is right despite the consequences. As an added bonus, you'll sleep better at night.

WALDO'S WINGTIPS

When dealing with a lack of integrity in those you lead or who are on your team:

- Confront appropriately. Put yourself in the other person's shoes before you say a thing. Hey, we've *all* messed up at some time or other in our careers.
- If it's your place to do so, apply immediate consequences that are proportionate to the offense.
- Provide coaching that can help the team member improve. Don't hit and run.
- Be consistent. Don't be one way with certain people and another with others. If your team sees your standards vary from person to person, you will lose *everyone's* trust and respect. Remember, justice wears a blindfold.

5

Lift Versus Drag

Find What Gives You Lift, and Jettison the Rest

THE SALTY SWEAT stings my eyes as I cross-check my engine instruments. Fuel flow, oil pressure, engine temperature—all look good. I check them again. And again. Everything has to be perfect. In seconds, the tower controller will clear me for the most exciting mission of my life: my first flight in the F-16.

In the backseat of the "D-model" training version of the F-16 jet fighter is my highly experienced instructor pilot and flight commander, Capt. John "Deke" Slaton. A decorated Iraq War veteran, meticulous instructor, and patient leader, he watches my every move. I trust him. He expects the best from me, as he should. We both know we could be flying in combat together a year from now, when I am deployed to an active duty Air Force base as a mission-qualified F-16 pilot. In the Air Force, we live by the saying "Fight like you train."

My left hand has a viselike grip on the bulky throttle with its numerous switches and buttons. My right hand curls around the stick that controls the elevator and ailerons. I rotate it quickly clockwise and then counterclockwise, testing the flight controls to make sure they operate smoothly. The stick moves only a few centimeters in any direction, since the F-16 is all about "fly by wire" technology. Electrical impulses send signals to the control services that help the plane fly—an amazingly sophisticated feat of aeronautical engineering. Thirty million dollars of machine, and *I* am at the controls. I feel like Hercules. I also can scarcely believe I'm actually going to fly this thing!

My quick but steady breathing echoes in my headset as I wait for the tower controller to clear me for takeoff. It feels like forever. I'm nervous but confident. I have chair flown this mission dozens of times in my head and in the simulator. Most important, Deke and I planned and briefed the flight in minute detail. From ground operations to area maneuvers to emergency procedures, I am ready for any contingency. But most of all, I'm ready, finally, to fly this jet on my own.

My headset crackles. "Viper two-one, this is Luke Tower. You are cleared for takeoff."

Deke calls out over the intercom, "OK, Waldo, you have the aircraft, buddy. Push it up!"

It's go time.

I thrust my feet forward to lock the brakes as I push up the engine to full power for what is called a static takeoff. Before I release the brakes, the engine instruments have to check within prescribed limits. Everything looks good. I double—check just to make sure. I release the brakes and am instantly flattened into the seat as the twenty thousand pounds of thrust kicks in. The acceleration is unreal as we gain speed: 150, 200, 250 knots. In seconds we're airborne. I raise the gear handle. I'm already at 300 knots, nearly 345 miles per hour. Deke yells out in the back, "Great Job, Waldo!"

And then it hits me: I'm flying the F-16!

Exactly two years later I would find myself strapped into another F-16, taking off on a very different mission. Nobody else was with me in the plane, but I wasn't flying solo. My wingmen and I were in combat over Iraq, in skies a lot less friendly than those over Phoenix, Arizona. Weighed down with two 370-gallon wing fuel tanks and a huge assortment of missiles and weapons systems, this jet was a lot heavier and less maneuverable than the one I flew in training. But the new configuration wasn't the only thing that weighed me down. Flying six hours at night through enemy skies, my fear, anxiety, and claustrophobia added to the weight I felt. But the mission had to get done.

Two flights in the F-16. Two completely different missions.

What helped determine the difference were the lift and the drag.

THE SCIENCE OF LIFT

Have you ever wondered how a thirty-five-thousand-pound F-16 combat-configured jet gets into the air? It's no easy feat. An abbreviated lesson in aerodynamics will help you understand how these amazing machines not only fly but perform superbly.

To overcome the force of gravity, you have to generate an opposing force greater than gravity. That force is *lift*. When the pressure of the air passing beneath the wings of an aircraft is greater than the pressure of the air above the wings, the plane will become airborne.

In order for it to accelerate and remain airborne, the F-16 must overcome any opposition to lift. This opposition is any aerodynamic force that resists the forward or upward motion of the jet and is known as *drag*. Every flight of every aircraft is an ongoing battle between the forces of lift and drag. A skilled pilot is essentially a great general of this battle. He, along with the flight computers present on modern-day jet fighters, minimizes drag and maximizes lift according to the desired path of the jet.

Fighter pilots have to deal with two kinds of drag: *induced drag* and *parasite drag*.

Induced drag is a natural byproduct of lift and is considered a "good drag," caused by the shape of the aircraft (wings, fuselage, and so on). While induced drag can be reduced in flight based on the position of the wings and rudders, it can never be fully eliminated. In flying, it comes with the territory.

Parasite drag is the opposite. It battles against the good drag, slowing the aircraft and hampering maneuverability. Any portion of the aircraft that does not create lift (landing gear, missiles, or external fuel tanks, for example) creates parasite drag. Some parasite drag, like the landing gear, is automatically eliminated once the jet takes flight and the gear is raised. Other parasite drag, like missiles or external fuel tanks, must be eliminated when its presence hinders necessary progress and lifesaving maneuverability.

Managing lift and drag is critical when flying in hostile skies. When evading missiles or engaging another fighter in close combat, one of the most critical things fighter pilots must instinctively do is "jettison their stores." That means getting rid of all the parasite drag hanging from the jet that is not critical to survival. Extra fuel tanks and missiles are all ditched. This reduces weight while simultaneously reducing drag, allowing the fighter to be more maneuverable and, hopefully, avoid getting shot down. There's an important lesson for business and life in this analysis.

WHAT IS DRAGGING YOU DOWN?

No matter how skilled or motivated you are, you're always going to have some degree of both parasite and induced drag in your life. And just like a fighter pilot, you must manage it and not let it hold you back from accomplishing your mission.

Let's look at parasite drag first. This is the drag that lies outside yourself. It's what "hangs" from your airframe.

The most obvious parasite drag is the negative relationships that sap your energy, pollute your airspace with negativity or pessimism, and give nothing in return. This drag can come in the shape of coworkers you hang out with in the break room, or peers you associate with on the weekend. You may call them friends, but they really aren't. They are the ones who possibly do drugs, badmouth their company and country, show disrespect to others, or lack integrity. These aren't wingmen; they're wing *nuts*! They may act as though they support you in your life but they're the first to tell you you're "not smart enough for that new job," that you "won't make it," or that you "really shouldn't be asking for that raise." They suck the life out of you and hold you back from reaching your highest potential. You must remove these people's influence from your life if you want to punch through your old flight ceiling.

Parasite drag also manifests itself in jobs, or even careers, that stifle your creativity or neglect your best skills. Right now, as you are reading these words, you may be stuck in a job that you literally feel is dragging you down. Until you find a way to jettison this drag, you'll not only wind up depressed and resentful, you'll put a concrete ceiling on your potential. Sure, it's risky to leave a secure job, especially in this uncertain economy. But I'm talking about reaching *new* heights here. *All growth comes with risk.*

Induced drag, on the other hand, comes *from you* and is completely *controlled by you*—and it's even harder to get rid of than parasite drag. It's your negative, counterproductive habits and self-limiting beliefs and fears—things you do that you know you shouldn't do. Do you have a private addiction to gambling, alcohol, or TV? Do you easily get distracted by non-mission-critical items, such as answering the phone when you don't need to or checking e-mail every five minutes when you should be working on a proposal? Do you spend more time filing your paperwork or talking to coworkers than discussing ways to improve your sales or management processes? At work, are you complacent, letting others take on added responsibilities while you shirk any task that isn't absolutely necessary? Or are you "all thrust and no vector," rushing around and looking busy but not really accomplishing all that much? Such attitudes can easily take you off the course of success. They will drag you down and keep you from going to the next level in your career and life.

Induced drag takes a lot more discipline and self-control to jettison. And unlike with parasite drag, you're probably not going to be able to release all of it. After all, sometimes you may not even be aware that these actions are dragging you down. It's tough to do, but if you want to break free of what's holding you back, you must release them.

JETTISON DRAG

What's dragging you down right now? Are you willing to ditch it so you can climb higher and be more maneuverable? Are you willing to look with clear eyes and let go of an unhealthy relationship, a habit of laziness, or a private addiction? If a bad job is weighing you down or a fear of failure is stopping you from starting a new business, are you willing to take a risk, step outside your comfort zone, and fly?

One of your primary objectives as a wingman in life is to gain lift and minimize drag so you can fly to new heights and gain the necessary flexibility to dodge the missiles of adversity that are launched at you. But you also want to be in the best possible position to support your wingmen. Your team member may be experiencing some challenges and may need you to step up and lend a wing.

WEATHERING THE STORM

No mission always has clear skies. Bad weather is inevitable, and sooner or later, the clouds and turbulence will come. This is when character and skill get put to the test. Pilots deal with storms in one of two ways: grin and bear it and take off, or abort the mission.

My wingmen and I have aborted many training missions where safety was a factor. Even in the military, there is no peacetime duty that requires unnecessary risks. But guess what? Sometimes we don't have a choice. This is particularly true in combat, where lives are literally on the line. For example, I remember taking off for several combat missions in Serbia in driving rain and gusty winds. It was stressful, and the drag (fear, anxiety, stress) was great, but my wingmen and I simply had to suck it up and get the job done. We had no choice but to reduce our induced drag.

Sooner or later, you're going to have a tough, dark day with thunderstorms and turbulence. You'll feel a lot of weight on your shoulders. Perhaps you'll lose a sale, miss out on that promotion, hear bad news from a friend, experience a health problem, or get into an argument with your boss. Even so, you may still need to give that product demo, make the cold call, run the board meeting, or tend to that patient. The job has to get done. Like a fighter pilot in combat, you may not always have the luxury of a choice.

THREE Rs FOR REACHING NEW HEIGHTS

So what do you do when you *must* fly under adverse conditions? Here are three ways you can maximize lift and minimize drag and still keep flying in tough environments.

Refocus

Focus on what you love. On my night combat missions when I would sense a claustrophobic panic attack coming on, I had a special contingency plan. I would open up my checklist and look down at a picture of my niece and nephew, Jennifer and Harrison. Looking at them got me focused on those I really loved and distracted me from my fear. *Love lifts; fear drags.*

It also got me focused on who *needed me*. It forced me to "think outside my cockpit" and got me out of my head. Looking at these photos gave meaning to my mission. What gives meaning to *your* mission? When you put yourself in a service mind-set, you'll instantly shift your perspective and gain courage. So focus on what gives lift to your life.

Want to find what gives you lift? Look at what drives your passion. Look at who needs you to perform. Look at the relationships and activities that get you excited and energized and ready to "push it up" in life. Then pursue them relentlessly. Seek what gives you life: your children, your friends and family, physical fitness, music, a pet, nature, trusted colleagues, your work, God—whatever it is.

Refuel

Fighter pilots have stringent rest requirements, and they must have twelve hours of uninterrupted rest time before they can fly. If not, they are grounded. The reason is simple: fatigue severely inhibits performance. No one can go nonstop and give 100 percent all the time. We need to give ourselves a break. Take time to refuel and rest.

Burnout is a leading culprit not just in lack of productivity in the workplace but in emotional stress, bad health, and a host of other ills. If you feel you are literally dragging, maybe it's time to step back and just take a break. Take a short vacation, get a massage, or sleep in one weekend. When I was based in Italy and flying missions into Serbia, I would occasionally take long hikes in the Italian Alps and just drink in the natural beauty surrounding me. It really helped me to relax and get recentered.

Don't worry if you have to put your work on hold for a short while. I guarantee, once you get back in the cockpit, your increased performance and efficiency will more than make up for the time you spent recharging your batteries.

Retool

Aircraft head into the hangars periodically for maintenance. Engines must get changed and systems upgraded. We all need a tune-up every so often—time to revamp our approach, sharpen our tools, and get a fresh perspective on things. If we don't upgrade our skills and rebalance our attitude, eventually we'll burn out our engine and crash. This might mean exercising, meditating, attending professional development seminars, or simply reading a book. Each of us retools in his or her own way.

Remember, *you* fly your aircraft and are at the controls. If something isn't working in your life, you need to take action and fix it. You, and no one else, are ultimately the pilot in command of your own career, and only you can take the action necessary to grow. There may be times when you won't be able to see how best to do this until you step back and take a closer look at the relationships, actions, and habits that define your flight path. Remember, your perspective can be limited. Sometimes it takes a wingman to check your six, perform a battle-damage check, and let you know it's time to get to the hangar and do some work on yourself. Don't hold back from asking a trusted partner to do a maintenance check on you—it's one of the best things you can do for yourself.

WINGMEN LIFT; WING NUTS DRAG

Jim Rohn, one of my favorite business philosophers, says, "Don't spend major time with minor people." If you want to be a high achiever, spend time with people who lift you up and challenge you. Share your days with wingmen who have the courage, credibility, and compassion to tell it like it is. They won't accept your excuses and will challenge you to grow. And they will also be your cheerleaders. Capt. Deke Slaton, my F-16 instructor, was like that. He both challenged and inspired me. We always had fun when we flew together. Having him in my backseat on my first F-16 flight gave me courage and confidence to take off.

So . . . how do you attract these people into your life? You be what you want to attract. You become a trusted wingman and *help others fly* to greater heights. You give your time, encouragement, and advice to others who need it. You become a "wing giver" to someone with a broken wing. You help dissipate their drag while lifting them up with your wings. For example, every week I try to go to lunch with someone new whom I can help. As a result, others always seem to be there to offer help when *I* need it. What goes around, comes around.

Bottom line: you must do the hard work to build your own character and develop relationships with others *before* expecting others to do the same for you. This is the core of leadership. For when you do this, the wingmen and partners you want in your life will naturally be attracted to you. They will feel comfortable coming to you for help, and you will quickly find yourself surrounded by people who lift *you* up. You get the most lift when you're giving lift.

PUSH YOURSELF; PULL OTHERS

When I first started flying combat missions, I was terrified most of the time. Most pilots were. For me, dealing with the fact that I was going to have to strap into the F-16 for four to six hours at a time, mostly at night, was all but unbearable. The fear of having a panic attack dragged me down, and I spent many days depressed and tense. Others could sense this in me, but I couldn't share it with anyone in the squadron. When things got really tough for me and I had a lot on my shoulders, I would pick up the phone and call my twin brother, Dave.

"I'm scared, Dave," I would say. "I don't know if I can fly today. I'm really stressed. Help me out, bro." It was humbling.

He would always respond eagerly. "Rob, you can do this. You did it before, and you'll do it again! Go make me proud. Be strong. You're a fighter pilot!"

Though he never said it in so many words, in essence what he was telling me was, "I believe in you."

He was my wingman. He pulled me up. He lifted me. With him, I knew I wasn't flying solo.

In these stressful times, where doubt and fear and anxiety are ever-present, we need people who can lift us up, not drag us down. We need *comrades of courage* who can pull us out of our dungeon of doubt. We need coworkers and loved ones, even strangers, who will give us the courage to strap on our jets, face our fears, and fly the tough missions.

We need partners at home and at work who are open to hearing three of the most important words in the English language: "I need help."

"Mayday! Mayday!" is the wingman's call to action.

Right now someone needs you to be her or his wingman. I hope you'll answer the call.

WALDO'S WINGTIPS

Here are five WingTips for maximizing lift and minimizing drag in your career:

- **Feed your mind with positive thoughts.** When Napoleon Hill was writing the classic *Think and Grow Rich*, he interviewed five hundred of the most successful people in the world at the time and compiled their common traits and characteristics. The practice of feeding the mind positive thoughts was one that came up every time.
- **Jettison the wing nuts in your career.** Every one of us bears the composite influence of the people we associate with the most. Make sure your "top five" are lifting you up, not dragging you down.
- **Join a mastermind group of people who are pushing it up.** Spend time with high achievers who are taking their life to the next level, but choose people with skills and insights different from yours. This way, you each can benefit from the others' unique expertise.
- **Mentor someone less experienced than you.** Take someone under your wing and encourage them, teach them, and lift them up. By lifting another, you add to your team of wingmen and build a stronger formation of partners. (Also, be willing to be mentored!)
- **Tighten down the rivets.** Induced drag is like the rivets on a jet: they hold the jet together, but if one sticks

out only one-sixteenth of an inch, it causes enormous drag when the jet is flying at high speed. "Tighten down your rivets" is another way of saying, "Take care of your life off the job." Don't neglect it. Tend to your spiritual, emotional, family, and physical needs and you'll fly a lot faster through life.

6

Break Right!

Give Mission-Critical Feedback When the Missiles Are Launched

IT's 12:30 A.M., and the moonless night sky appears peaceful and serene. The only sound I hear is the steady hum of the F-16's jet engine. I'm flying 350 knots at twenty-two thousand feet, on a combat mission in Serbia during Operation Allied Force. My wingmen are five miles off my nose and five miles in trail. We are all scanning our radar for enemy aircraft, surface-to-air missiles (SAMs), and radar activity. Over half our time is spent looking for unseen threats and "checking six"—covering our wingmen's blind spots.

Suddenly, my wingman's voice blares over the radio, "Break right, break right! Missile launch your five o'clock!" My heartbeat ramps up, and I feel a surge of adrenaline run down my neck as my fight-or-flight reflex kicks in. I bank the aircraft ninety degrees to the right and pull back on the stick as hard as I can. The G forces flatten me into the seat as my G-suit instantly inflates with a rush of air. The pressure on my chest and legs almost squeezes the air right out of my lungs.

Just as I've practiced, I lower the nose, jettisoning chaff to help break the radar lock, and twist my head and neck around to get a visual of the missile. I realize that not one but two missiles are hurtling toward me at twice the speed of sound. The smoke-and-fire plume of their exhaust is ominous, flaring up through the night sky like Roman candles on the Fourth of July. I finish the maneuver to avoid the missiles' flight path, and they explode into fireballs a scant thousand feet from the aircraft. And just like that, it's over. For the first time ever, I have defeated a real, no-joke threat on my life. It feels like a dream.

But before I can savor the victory, I realize I am now "low and slow"—a perfect target for more SAMs and anti-aircraft artillery (AAA). Fear grips me again as I rocket sky-ward to gain altitude as tracers of AAA appear all around me. I frantically search for my wingmen. I need to reestablish mutual support. I have no clue where my flight lead is, and I feel like a baby antelope on the African plains, surrounded by lions. I call out on the radio, "Two's blind, state position."

Capt. John "Yoda" Pearse, my flight lead, calls out, "Two, I'm on your nose, six miles at twenty thousand feet!"

I refocus in that direction, adjust my radar, and exhale relief as I spot my wingman on my radar, a bright green square on my multifunction display (MFD). I reestablish a five-mile trail position (the night-flying standard) and continue the mission. I am now "tied" to my flight lead, and mutual support is established.

I survived. *We* survived—but only as a team working together.

Definitely not a typical day in the life of a fighter pilot, that mission changed my life forever. You see, not every mission is full of glory and winning. Sometimes it's just about coming back. Survival is when you're focused on the competition or threat, and winning is when you're focused on the target. When the missiles come, it's nearly impossible to focus on the target. And let me tell you, the job of surviving is almost never fun, especially when it involves forty-foot missiles full of explosives.

Now, if you look closely at the combat mission I described, it's clear what made survival possible. Without hesitation, when I heard "Break right!" I *took my wingman's advice and acted*. I applied evasive maneuvering procedures and took fierce, tactical action—on trust alone. Also, my wingman never left me. He maintained situational awareness and talked my eyes onto him.

You are flying missions every day at work. They aren't as intense as combat (although in some ways they may appear to be), yet the stakes are high nonetheless. The key not just to surviving but also to *winning* these missions is trusting your wingmen—your coworkers, partners, collaborators, friends, or spouse. You must trust these partners when it really counts, because in the heat of battle, you'll never be able to see all the missiles coming at you. This measure of trust—even more than self-trust—breeds the highest form of confidence.

I may have strapped into the cockpit of an F-16 by myself on sixty-five combat missions, but I was never flying solo. I always had my wingmen—my trusted, reliable partners in the air and on the ground. They helped me not only to survive but to succeed.

WINNERS NEVER FLY SOLO

Winners always fly as a team, for though we may manage to survive on our own, we win together. When the missiles come, you always have a choice: you either control the situation or are controlled by it. I'm not referring to mere self-confidence here. You can't control every circumstance; in fact, *most* things will always lie outside your individual control. It's a fact we all sooner or later must accept humbly rather than fight with false bravado. It's life. Greater control and confidence is a function of a trustworthy team of supporters who have your back at all times and alert you the moment they see something threatening you or the team's mission.

I remember sitting with a few hundred of my squadron mates during our intelligence in-briefing at Aviano Air Base in Italy. We were part of Operation Allied Force, sent to defeat the brutal regime of Slobodan Milosevic. A huge map of Yugoslavia was projected on a screen. Missile systems were everywhere. Pilots were getting SA-3 and SA-6 missiles shot at them every day, and some pilots were even shot down. The enemy was skilled. This was no joy ride—you could sense the fear, tension, and anxiety.

But there was also a sense of calm in the room that is hard to explain. When I looked around, I saw people I trusted. I saw men and women who were the best-trained pilots, maintenance crews, and intelligence officers in the world. I felt their focus, commitment, integrity, trust, and dedication to one another. We knew we were ready for battle. We knew we could trust each other to call out "Break right!" when the missiles came. We were warriors with a mission.

They were my wingmen. They inspired me and gave me courage. They made all the difference. I wouldn't be flying alone, and I knew that together, we would be successful in our mission—just as you and your wingmen will lead each other to success.

ONE TEAM, ONE MISSION

If there was one thing that got hammered into me more than anything else in my military training, it was the concept of teamwork and trust. In fact, unity was the prevailing theme in our training, not to mention in our deployments. Everyone was a partner. We knew our role and how it fit precisely into the big picture, realizing that we were only as strong as the weakest member of our squadron. The mission was a combination of all our efforts, from the fighter pilots to the maintenance crews to the intelligence officer to the life support staff. Anyone who tried to accomplish the mission on their own eventually failed. We had to work together.

Can you imagine if this type of mentality and commitment were present in your work environment? What if you knew that when you looked left and right you could implicitly trust your coworker, boss, associate, or vendor?

The old paradigm that maverick leaders and solo entrepreneurs set the bar is outdated and no longer relevant in today's economy. While self-leadership is critical to any business endeavor, the only way to maximize your potential, fulfill your mission—and the mission of your organization—and reach new heights is with the help of others, through authentic partnerships. Sometimes these partners show up where you least expect them.

Imagine arriving at the office with mud on your shoes and sopping wet clothes. Your car blew a tire on the way in, and when you got out to take a look, a pickup truck hit the puddle next to you. After enduring jokes from the receptionist and anyone else who sees you in your "fine" business attire, you get to your office and find that the printed and collated copies of your big presentation for the upcoming trade show were delivered on schedule—bound upside down and in the wrong order. Throw in your two junior staff members complaining about the raises they didn't get, and you can start to feel the steam billowing from your ears. Not exactly missiles, but enough to make you feel as if you were hurtling to Earth.

Enter your wingman, Marge, an inside sales manager who is your partner on several accounts. She closes your office door, lets you rant a little while, and then sets you at ease and gets you back on the right flight path. You've got battle damage and are calling out Mayday, and she's in the perfect position to help you stay airborne and not let you crash.

Someone in the print shop owes her a favor—she'll be able to get your copies fixed in time. And the two whining staff members? Marge points out that one got a raise just two months ago, and the other is up for a performance review in a week. You'll be able to give him a pay bump then if it's merited. Problems solved.

As your blood pressure inches back down, Marge suggests that you pull a change of clothes from your gym bag and give your suit to the cleaners in the lobby of the building, which offers one-hour service. "Now, Phil, let's talk about the Acme account," says Marge, pulling out a pad and pen. "We have that big presentation, and we need a slam dunk to win the business. Here's what I think we should do. . . ."

In minutes your trusted wingman has helped you "break right" and avoid catastrophe. She was a perfect "chase ship" and didn't let you hit the ground. You're back in formation and on your way to victory, and your boss is all smiles, too.

CALLING ALL WINGMEN

Are you even aware of the wingmen at your office? Perhaps they're the ones behind the scenes—unsung heroes quietly committed to the job and making a difference day in and day out. Are you backing each other up, checking for missile launches, and calling out "Break right!" when necessary? Most important, when your wingmen tell you to break, do you trust them enough to heed the call? Or do you tend to question them, doubt their credibility, or even resent them for advising you what to do? Remember, real leaders accept and even seek feedback, even though it may not be much fun in the moment.

Have you ever been in a situation in which you've worked hard for something—a new project at work, a promotion, a marriage—and one of your wingmen pulls you aside and gently explains that you aren't quite ready, perhaps not even *right*, for the responsibility? Maybe you were criticized about some very personal issues or told that to improve your chances of winning the new client you needed to improve your communication skills, change your professional attire, and even cut back on your drinking. Your wingman has spotted bogeys bearing down on you and is warning you to break right before serious trouble ensues. Is he or she worth listening to? Although it feels like a personal slap in the face, the choice you make in that moment is critical: heed the call and avoid getting shot down, or ignore it and risk major disaster.

Being a wingman is all about trust. Trust yourself first, then your team. Trust implies mutual respect, confidence, and compassion. Not everyone can be your wingman, and that's why you must choose carefully. After all, who wants to take criticism from someone we don't trust?

Being a wingman also implies shared responsibility. When you hear "Break right!" you not only need to listen carefully (and act), you need to be willing to call it out as well. This takes more courage than you might think. But if you really care about someone and consider her your wingman, you have to do what's right to help this person grow. After all, no one likes to give unfavorable feedback, tell someone he has a problem, or take the keys from a friend who shouldn't be driving. But consider the potential cost to your wingman if you *don't* act.

MUTUAL SUPPORT LEADS TO MISSION SUCCESS

Every day, you are placed in situations in which you might need wingmen to help you gain perspective and fly more effectively. Wingmen help you with perspective because it's easy to get so focused on a project, or so comfortable with your habits, that you lose sight of the big picture. You can be flying with blinders on without ever knowing it—not a great situation when the missiles start coming.

A good wingman will recognize when you aren't function-ing at the highest level of performance. Why? Because they know you and they care. They see your blind spots and give you some perspective when your vision is limited. A good wingman won't hesitate to call out "Break right!" to help you refocus on the mission and perhaps avoid a dangerous problem lurking at your six.

Honest, ego-free, two-way communication is critical. After all, sustained success requires fast, accurate decisions. To get these decisions and their consequent actions right, you must rely on training and instinct. And when these two resources are limited by stress, lack of skills, or task overload, you have your wingmen there to build the picture and still succeed at the mission.

The key to establishing all wingman partnerships is self-leadership and accountability.

Self-leadership is necessary for the highest level of trust to exist between partners. If you know that your partner is always prepared, you can breathe easy, confident that she will do her part every time. Of course, the same has to be true of you. If *you* are the weak link, it will be difficult for others to stay ready to watch your back, since you aren't prepared to watch theirs. Not only must your partner be prepared to do her part in fulfilling the mission, she must be prepared to help you do yours as well. This is the foundation of what I call *wingmanship*—the unfaltering commitment to a wingman relationship. Imagine how I would feel walking to the jet on a combat mission and wondering if my wingman was truly ready.

Consider the last time you launched into a shared endeavor with people who were not prepared. Wasn't the pressure on you that much higher? If you were prepared and they weren't, didn't you feel a sense of injustice—even anger—toward these so-called partners? For a wingman relationship to exist, there must be the highest degree of self-leadership so that the highest degree of trust is instinctual. There will be times when the slightest hesitation means death—whether of a prospective relationship, an account, a project, or a job. The mutual trust of a wingman relationship makes it possible to avoid this fate.

Accountability is the other primary ingredient of a wingman relationship. First, great wingmen "chair fly." They are highly trained and prepare relentlessly for every mission. They take courageous action to do the right thing. They provide emotional and intellectual support when you call for help. They identify stressors and take personal responsibility to intervene. They listen actively. And they know when to ask for help from you. All these activities require a high level of accountability that refuses to cater to the ego. It's one thing for an ill-prepared, unreliable coworker to call you out. How does that feel? But it's another feeling altogether when a reliable, well-prepared coworker calls you out on something that is questionable or misdirected. Clearly, the latter is easier to receive. When this standard is established up front in your work partnerships, the instinctive behavior of every person moves the mission forward, making progress—even immediate progress—possible every day.

SECURING YOUR BEST WINGMEN

The process of identifying the wingmen around you begins with *observation*. Look around and identify the people in your professional life who have rock-solid integrity and are consistently *on time and on target*. Yes, they may be your friends, and they may be people you interact with regularly. They may also be people you have only watched from a distance. Don't make the mistake of shrinking the pool of potential wingmen to people you already know. If the best wingmen are outside your circle, then step outside. *Think outside the cockpit.* Find the best wingmen possible for your formation. The higher the standards you set for your wingmen, the higher your standards will be, and the higher you'll be able to climb.

The next step to establishing your wingmen partnerships is to establish mutually agreeable "contracts" and relationship expectations. The best way to do this is to ask your wingmen to be brutally honest with you when they see you getting complacent or lacking accountability. Don't accept yes-men and -women into your formation. Solicit feedback and encourage each other to participate mutually in your professional development. A good technique is to ask, "How can I become better?" rather than "What am I doing wrong?" Finally, don't get defensive when receiving feedback that may not be favorable. Keep an open mind—good wingmen will challenge you to grow and stretch beyond your comfort zones.

As you continually seek to build and nurture partnerships in your life, set your sights high and have a mind-set that seeks to serve others as you would want to be served. If you see a wingman struggling with clipped wings, don't let him crash. Be what I call a *wing giver*. True, you may have to lend your wings at times, and this can temporarily keep you from soaring as high as you might. But have faith that when the time is right, this wingman, or perhaps another, will be sure to help you fly to new heights.

In the Air Force, one of the three core values is "service before self." It serves as a constant reminder that as a military organization, we are here to serve. What if everyone in your organization or local community were committed to service? Imagine the productivity and heightened morale that would result.

Always be willing to give a wing when you see a wingman in need. Give your courage, support, and hope. Don't hold back. And finally, never leave your wingman. In the end, you'll get what you have given.

WALDO'S WINGTIP

This week, take a risk. Give someone you work with a "battle damage check" and provide some feedback that person may not want to hear even though he or she *needs* to hear it. Step out of your comfort zone and make a difference for that person. Remember, the key here is to operate from a place of mutual respect and commitment to the overall health of this wingman and your team. Be careful not to judge, and focus on the behavior, not the person. And finally, offer some support and coaching. Don't just snipe and run. Stay in that coworker's formation and be a resource.

7

Lose Sight, Lose Fight

Wingmen Keep You Focused and on Course

"JUST REMEMBER, WALDO, if things get out of control, just stay visual."

These were my wingman's last words to me as I headed to my F-16 to do my walk-around inspection. I repeated them over and over in my head: "Just stay visual." Simple enough, right?

I had already flown more than forty combat missions and was relatively experienced in the world of aerial combat, but I was still nervous. As my wingman and flight lead, Capt. Rob "Koz" Kosciusko would lead me to the target. I just had to trust him.

I loved flying with Koz. Not only was he a great instructor pilot, he was a friend—a great friend, in fact. We spent a lot of time together outside the squadron, and I trusted his judgment on more than just flying. We even shared the same career path. Both first-assignment instructor pilots (FAIPs), we were stationed in many of the same bases. And when it came time to choose a follow-on assignment, we both selected the F-16.

We followed each other to Kunsan Air Base in South Korea and then finally to Shaw Air Force Base in South Carolina. Koz was probably the closest wingman I had in my entire Air Force career, and I felt damn lucky to have him in my personal formation.

But we were very different. Koz had golden hands; mine were only silver on a good day. The guy was an amazing pilot, and he progressed up through the flying ranks faster than any other fighter pilot I knew. No matter how bad the weather or intense the threat, Koz always maintained a laser focus. He knew the nearest divert fields, was keenly aware of the fuel and weapons state of each of his wingmen, and, most important, knew *where* they were at all times. He never lost sight.

I felt safe when we flew together, so when we took off on a two-ship mission deep into hostile Serbian territory, I knew I was in good hands. All I had to do was just hang on and not lose sight of him.

We established our twenty-mile oval "cap" in the southern part of Serbia (close to the city of Pristina) and began "sanitizing" the airspace by searching for SAMs and radar sites. The weather was perfect: a cloudless blue sky with twenty-plus miles of visibility. My job was simple: stay a mile and a half to two miles line-abreast with Koz at all times—an ideal position for working our radars in unison should an air threat appear. The formation also helped us maintain visual contact so we could check each other's six for unseen threats. Minimal radio communication was required, so every maneuver and turn had to be done through visual signals such as "wing rocks," in which the lead aircraft rocks his wing in the desired direction of the turn.

Once in the cap, we quickly found our rhythm. Every twenty miles or so, we turned 180 degrees in our cap and flew the opposite direction. No threat or radar activity was showing up, and out of boredom I started sightseeing, exploring the little towns outside Pristina, twenty thousand feet beneath us. I also buried my head in the cockpit and started working my radar outside my briefed responsibilities. My cross-check slowed. I became complacent. Instead of checking Koz's six and staying visual, I blew him off—after all, there were no threats to worry about.

A minute or so passed, and I looked outside expecting to find Koz in anticipation of a wing rock to reverse our direction. Instead, he was gone.

My eyes darted up and down and side to side as I searched frantically for him. I gazed into the clear blue sky, trying to find the dark-gray speck of his F-16, but saw only blue horizon. Five seconds passed . . . then ten, fifteen. Where was he? Had he already turned? Was he underneath me? Did he get shot down by a missile I could have warned him about if I had been checking his six?

Every second that passed further damaged the integrity of the formation as we potentially drifted farther and farther apart. My heartbeat quickened. We were not a unified team anymore. There was no mutual support.

Then, I had to make the radio call that no fighter pilot ever wants to make. It's a call that often demonstrates carelessness, lack of skill, and poor discipline. I squeezed the mike with my left thumb and reluctantly called out, "Two's blind."

I felt like a loser. What would Koz think of me? Would he be disappointed or even angry? Would he think I was incompetent? *What the heck is Waldo doing? Why can't he keep sight of me? How many times did I tell him not to lose sight?* Who wants to go into combat with someone who can't even stay visual?

Although I had lost sight of Koz, I prayed he hadn't lost sight of *me*. The Serbian missile operators on the ground would love that.

It seemed an eternity before Koz answered. "Two, come right thirty degrees, I'll be on your nose for three miles, slightly high."

Whew! Koz came through again. *How'd he do that?* I thought to myself.

He talked my eyes onto him, and I could feel the tension dissipate as we got back into position. We were back on course, flying, as we say, the "same way, same day."

Fortunately, the rest of the mission was uneventful, and you can bet that my eyes never left Koz's jet and his six o'clock. During the debriefing, Koz asked why I went blind, and I was straight with him. He was my wingman, and I owed him the hard truth. I told him I was too busy messing with the radar and sightseeing and thus failed to check his six as I should have. And while he didn't criticize me, I could sense the disappointment in his eyes. I had let him down, failed in my primary role as a wingman: not to lose sight. Koz didn't need to remind me how hazardous it was for me to go blind, especially in combat. If the threat had been severe that day, we both would have been sitting ducks. I never forgot how I felt that day and vowed I would never again lose sight of my wingman.

THE INTEGRITY OF YOUR EYES

We have a saying in the fighter pilot world: "Lose sight, lose fight." In every combat and training mission, rule number one is never to lose sight of your wingmen. If you do, you sacrifice the integrity and capabilities of the entire formation. You also have to keep sight of the threat, be it a ground target you're attacking or an enemy fighter you're engaging. The eyes are a fighter pilot's most lethal weapons, which is why most pilots are required to have exceptional vision. It takes tremendous discipline, concentration, and focus to maintain sight in the heat of battle, where there are a multitude of distractions.

In cases where a wingman does indeed lose sight, it's imperative that he call it out quickly. There is no room for ego. The key is to admit the error, fix it, and continue the mission.

Staying Visual in Business

The critical importance of staying visual and not losing sight of your team in business can't be overstated. Let's first do a quick walk-around inspection of your organization. Have you ever worked for a manager whom you rarely saw? Maybe he shut himself away in his office, never to emerge and work with his team. Or maybe he connected with you only once a quarter during a periodic review, or you heard his voice only on a monthly conference call. How much did you trust that person? When you called out Mayday, he probably couldn't even hear you, or maybe he was just MIA. How did that make you feel?

What about the supervisor who always seems to be available and willing to share her time and advice? Perhaps you need her to visit that big account with you or coach you on your sales presentation, and she delivers big-time. Her office door is open, and she's on time and on target—always ready and willing to coach. What do you think about her? I bet you trust this person.

Regional managers, supervisors, and internal staff need to see and be seen with their wingmen. E-mails are good ways to communicate, but sometimes you just have to shake hands in person, see each other face-to-face, and openly offer your help and support.

In a large organization with many departments, connecting across organizational silos builds an appreciation of what each entity does. But in most companies, IT has no idea what finance does or what challenges it faces. Sales shies away from engineering, and marketing never touches base with HR unless it has to. But in those organizations where they do keep sight of each other, observe each other in action, and understand each other's processes, trust develops. And when trust is built, performance rises. Bottom line: you need to feel confident that when you call on your wingmen to get a job done, they'll be flying with you "same way, same day."

What about your vendors, partners, or customers? Are they keeping sight of you, and are you keeping sight of them?

If you've been to one of my programs, you may still have one of my gold and silver "Never Fly Solo, Wingman" teamwork coins. My clients love these coins, which symbolize the mission to win as one unified team. I had a great vendor out of New Jersey who supplied these coins to me for three years, and we developed a great relationship. After a while, though, we just lost touch. When a new coin supplier from northern California pitched me on his coins, guess what? I listened. He wound up being a really nice sales rep, and he developed a custom "Wingman" coin for me at a better price than my previous vendor's. Here's the thing: I probably never would have entertained this new vendor's call if my current vendor had kept in touch with me.

Never take for granted the relationships you have with your current suppliers and partners. In today's business, sad as it sounds, it's "here today, gone tomorrow." You never know what's going to happen. As the old saying goes, "out of sight, out of mind." And once out of sight, you will lose the fight.

Today, with the tough competition out there and rapidly changing demands of prospects and clients, you can't afford not to be seen or heard by your current partners and customers.

LOST WINGMAN

There are times when pilots fly in very close proximity (about three feet) in a formation called "fingertip." We do this when the weather gets really bad or if a wingman loses navigation ability or has some other type of system malfunction. Flying in fingertip provides mutual support and minimizes the tasks for the pilot experiencing the problem. The lead aircraft guides the wingman to the target or back to the airfield to land.

But if the weather gets so bad that the wingman can't even see the aircraft he's flying off of, he should then switch to instrument, turn away from the last known position of the other aircraft, and call out "Lost wingman." While this can be quite confusing and disorienting for the wingman who is lost, it's critical for maintaining safety. The flight lead's job is to stay in contact with the lost wingman, get rejoined on him again (in clear skies), or make sure air traffic control can get him on the ground safely.

In your personal life, have you ever gone "lost wingman" on a friend or wingman? You haven't seen this person in a while, he doesn't return your calls, or you've simply lost touch? One minute you're flying on his wing, and then suddenly he disappears. How did that make you feel? Maybe the lost wingman is *you*. You get so wrapped up in your work or life's challenges that you lose contact with those partners, colleagues, and peers most important to you.

CALLING OUT WHEN YOU'VE LOST SIGHT

The scenario is quite common. Sometimes the weather in our lives gets pretty bad and we can't see beyond our own cockpit. Financial, health, or family issues take over, and we lose sight of our wingmen or get knocked off course. We're flying along, everything's going peachy, and then suddenly it all goes dark. Can you relate? Perhaps you were laid off from your job. Maybe you lost a huge contract to a competitor after working on it for months, or maybe you got passed over for the promotion you put in for. Maybe you're struggling through a divorce or a personal tragedy or illness you can't shake. You crawl into your shell and disappear for a while. If no one checks in on you, they won't even realize you're not around.

You've got to be able to call out "Lost wingman" or "Two's blind" to your wingmen! If not, you're risking the relationship and your ability to land safely. Moreover, a good wingman will get you visual again (just as Koz did for me) and won't let you go "blind" or "lost wingman" in the first place. Sometimes you can't navigate for yourself and you need a wingman to help you get your bearings back. The hitch is that you can't call out "Lost wingman!" and expect to be led (or even *found*, for that matter) if you haven't already established relationships with wingmen.

But if you hold on and trust the judgment of the wingmen you have already allowed into your life, these people can keep you airborne until the clouds clear. Like Koz, they can talk your eyes back into position and lead you on their wing back to safer airspace. The truth is, with a good wingman, you're never really lost.

Here are five ways to make sure you keep sight of your most trusted wingmen and never get lost, no matter what flight path you're traveling on:

1. Make a list of your top twenty or so business contacts you wish to stay in touch with. Write down the name, address, phone number, e-mail, and organization for each. Now make a similar list, this time of your twenty *most trusted* friends and partners.

2. At least once a week, have a meal or a cup of coffee with a wingman from each of these groups. This is the time to be open, share challenges, ask for help, and, most of all, offer a wing. The person you're talking to may be "tumbleweed" (i.e., lost and without a clue) and may need your help, too.

3. If you can't meet in person, call at least every month or two just to check in. Carry the numbers around with you on a notepad or store them in your computer or handheld device so you can call when you're out.

4. Mentor a new wingman as often as you can. This doesn't have to be anything more formal than a lunch meeting and a few e-mails or phone calls to follow up. Do this

without any expectation of a business referral or other return favor.

5. When fighter pilots practice maneuvering in close fingertip formation, it's called "wingwork." It hones our skills and gets us used to maneuvering as one unified formation. You must do the same. Get out there in the real world and work in formation with your wingmen. Don't just network— "wingwork," with the focus on the other person. Be seen, and don't let your prospects, peers, and community lose sight of you.

BEWARE OF DISTRACTIONS DISGUISED AS OPPORTUNITIES

Henry David Thoreau once said, "In the long run, people hit only what they aim at." He was onto something. The key word here is "aim." Aim requires focus, and lack of focus is often the main culprit in a failed mission. Vision without focus leads to chaos. Lose sight, lose fight.

Most of us have a decent visual fix on where we are going. But in my experience, it's a rare thing when someone has the disciplined focus to stay consistently on target and accomplish the mission. This is where wingmen can help.

Think about it: You're entrenched in writing an incredible sales proposal, and the phone rings. Or you're practicing your sales pitch to that major prospect, and an e-mail pops up demanding an immediate response. Or you just sat down to plan tomorrow's schedule, and your friend calls to discuss a relationship issue.

One second, you're focused on the right action; the next, you're off target. These "opportunities" are merely distractions trying to veer you off course. What you do in these moments is critical. A few quick questions can help keep you on the flight path. First of all, if you don't see a clear upside to the "opportunity," be sure it isn't a plea (veiled or not) for you to be a good wingman and help sort out the problem. If it's a wingman in need, it may warrant a calculated deviation from your flight path. Can you ask the person to bring it up at a more convenient time for you—say, after work or over lunch? Is it a "quick fix"—something you can handle right now in, oh, a minute or less? Or do you see a long conversation looming, with no real benefit to either of you in sight?

And this is where a good wingman can help most. A good wingman keeps you accountable to the mission and corrects you back to your course. If you sense that an "opportunity" is a distraction in disguise, you may want to approach your wingman for some advice and ask something like "Hey Lisa, what's your take on X?" Take notes, and if warranted, challenge her with rebuttals.

You can't always blow off everything other than the task at hand. But if you are serious about success, you and your wingmen must have your mission priorities straight. While you may lose sight of them in the moment, hopefully your wingmen will not. Thus, you'll never go too far off course.

Sure, you can go for it on your own. But sustained success requires sustained focus. You mustn't lose sight of the target, while keeping an eye out for any obstacles in the way, including threats and potential distractions. This is possible only if you fly with your wingmen in sight. That way, you can build a much bigger picture of your mission than a single pair of eyes can encompass, and your chances of success go way up.

WALDO'S WINGTIP

Keeping Sight of Your Goals

When the "missiles" of the business world come at you, you may get stressed, anxious, and fearful. This is normal. Nobody ever wants to fail or see their dreams shot down. Under these conditions, it's easy to get disheartened and unmotivated. When this happens, don't pull back the throttle of your commitment. Resist the sometimes subtle urge to pull back! In tough times (like combat), it's even more critical that you push it up and remember what—and who— you are fighting for. You have to refocus on what your goals are. To keep your goals at the forefront, write them out and keep them visible. Make them as specific as you can, and read them out loud every day. Put photos of those you love and of your passions next to the goals. If you lose sight of the goals—and, more important, if you lose sight of what gives meaning to your mission—you will lose the fight. Keeping sight of your goals will give you the courage and the strength of will to stay committed until you succeed.

8

Situational Awareness

Effective Communication Builds Trust

THE FLOODLIT TARMAC at Prince Sultan Air Base, Saudi Arabia, is a beehive of activity as my wingmen and I walk toward the ground crew. Climbing into our sleek F-16 jets, we conduct our preflight checks for this five-hour night combat mission into Iraq.

Our call sign is "Viper 11," and we are part of a multistrike package of fourteen aircraft responsible for taking out an SA-3 surface-to-air missile site just outside Najaf in southern Iraq. Intelligence briefed us that the SAMs are active, as are multiple antiaircraft artillery sites. It's going to be intense.

The powerful turbines whine as we taxi toward the runway. Capt. Dieter "Deetz" Barheis, a weapons school graduate and a talented fighter pilot, checks us in on the radios.

"Viper flight, check."

"Two" . . . "Three" . . . "Four," we respond with perfect timing, and one by one, we take off northward into a star-filled moonless sky.

I've flown this route two dozen times before and know the way by heart. But tonight, I have no idea just how dark it is about to get.

We hit the KC-135 tanker to top off our fuel and change radios to the planned frequency. With only thirty miles till we reach the Iraqi border, I have barely five minutes to run through my combat checklist. Radar and transponder set, missile cooled, fuel tanks feeding, and air-to-air system configured, I am ready to cross the border. The only thing left to do is move my master arm switch to "hot." Three minutes pass, and I realize Deetz hasn't checked in on me over the radios. Screaming toward the enemy border, all I hear is silence.

I make a quick call to check on my wingmen: "Two's up." Nothing.

I double-check the frequency I wrote down in the pre-flight brief—233.9—and make another call. Still nothing. *Where are my wingmen?* Things are starting to get very dark.

I quickly refer to my checklist for radio-out procedures and check my connections, radio circuit breakers, and switches to make sure everything is operating properly. Am I on the right frequency? Is my radio broken? I then remember to cross-check my instruments. It's obvious I'm way behind my wingmen. My airspeed has dropped fifty knots, and I'm three hundred feet off my last assigned altitude. I can't even remember what my heading is supposed to be. I become "task saturated," a pilot's term for being overloaded and overwhelmed by a task. To make things worse, I can't even find my wingmen on my radar, and I have no idea where they are. A sense of dread overtakes me. I am now flying solo.

As I hurtle toward the Iraqi border, my anxiety ramps up. My inexperience is catching up with me. I am losing situational awareness (SA) fast. With no radio contact and only a general idea of where I am in the vast, pitch-black sky, I compile a mental checklist of my plight as several daunting contingencies run though my head: *What if I lose my engine? What happens if I'm engaged by ground fire? How can I call for help? Do my wingmen even know I'm not on their frequency?*

My entire focus shifts from supporting the mission to fixing this communication problem. I have no mutual support, no radios, and no clue. I'm "tumbleweed." If I don't get my SA back fast and link up with my wingmen, I'll have to abort the mission. My wingmen will have one less pilot to support the mission. Even worse, if this debacle winds up being my fault, I'll have to explain it all in the debriefing—*if* I make it back.

I bark to myself as if someone will hear me, "C'mon. Will somebody please check me in?"

Suddenly, my backup VHF radio blares with the stern voice of Deetz.

"Two! Come up frequency 239.9!"

I immediately change frequencies, realizing I wrote down the wrong UHF frequency in the preflight briefing! Worse, I realize I forgot to use the backup VHF radio to ask my wingmen to confirm the UHF frequency. This was standard procedure. I had screwed up royally.

I'm way out of position now and reluctantly tell Deetz that I am "blind" (no radar contact), and he updates his position to me. Under his guidance, I turn forty-five degrees to the right, adjust my radar sweep, and wonder how incompetent he must think I am. I am relieved as I pick him up on my radar, ten miles off my nose at twenty thousand feet. He checks us in once again.

"Vipers, check!"

We respond in a crisp monotone cadence: "Two" . . . "Three" . . . "Four."

Crossing the Iraqi border as a team, we arm our weapons. Viper flight is now marching to the same beat, "same way, same day"—a synchronized formation with a detailed flight plan and a mission objective. Our radar and radios link us together. We have situational awareness. We are ready for battle—no thanks to me. All thanks to my wingmen.

Looking back on this stressful mission, it was a single act that changed everything for me. One second I was calm, confident, and mission-ready; the next, I was in the dark, afraid, and full of doubt—a "second-guesser," flying solo with no situational awareness. But with a simple check-in on the radio and the reassuring sound of my experienced flight lead, I was back in the game, with my confidence and SA high once again.

TUMBLEWEED

Nobody likes being "in the dark." The mind can play terrible games when you find yourself operating in a communication vacuum; indeed, the most carefully laid plans can be undermined, even blown sky high, amid the corrosive doubt brought on by poor communication. This is particularly true in combat.

The complete opposite of being in the dark is having high situational awareness. SA is the very lifeblood of a mission, and it's a by-product of knowing where you and your wingmen are, where you're going, and all the variables that can affect the mission (weather, divert fields, threats, fuel state, status of wingmen, and so on). When your SA is high, you can adapt to changes quickly and maintain mission effectiveness. Without it, you're useless.

This anxious feeling of confusion and helplessness brought on by an emergency, a threat, a procedural error, or, most important, a rapidly changing environment, is what fighter pilots refer to as "tumbleweed." Picture a tumbleweed blowing aimlessly across the plains, at the mercy of the wind, destination unknown. When you are tumbleweed in a jet fighter, that's exactly how you feel. Adrift in the sky and with no situational awareness, you are of no value to the mission or the team. Your only thought is to get back on track and, most important, find your way back to your wingmen.

Radio communication is the most critical way to build SA in combat. When all else fails, it can save your life. However, going "dark"—not hearing (and thus not knowing) exactly what is happening in a situation—can reduce even a seasoned combat pilot to a powerless, ineffective second-guesser. On that night in Iraq, a simple lapse on my part cut communication to my wingmen and almost threw our entire mission into disarray. These lapses of communication can wreak havoc in business.

MISSION BRIEFING

Good communication has to be planned. The problem is that most organizations have terrible communication plans—or none at all.

A Web poll conducted by the Computing Technology Industry Association found that of more than a thousand people who took the poll, nearly 28 percent pointed to "poor communication" at the beginning of a project as the leading cause of project failure.[1]

What set things straight on the mission in Iraq was that my wingmen and I conducted a pre-mission briefing, in which we discussed a communication plan along with other contingency plans. Thus, we knew in advance how to handle communication challenges and other possible mishaps. In the fog and chaos of combat, when the unexpected happens and the stress level is high, it's easy to forget mission-critical items. Preparing for the unexpected through a contingency plan during the briefing minimizes chaos and doubt and keeps the entire formation focused on the task at hand.

A good mission briefing:

- starts on time and ends on time
- communicates the mission's overall objectives
- delegates specific responsibilities to each wingman
- explains the expected environment where the mission will take place
- highlights threats and discusses tactics for defeating them
- details specific procedures to ensure constant two-way communication, including a backup plan should communication fail (called a "lost comm" plan)
- reviews contingency plans and emergency procedures

The mission briefing sets standards of performance so that *everyone* knows exactly what is expected of each team member. Coordinated and briefed by the flight lead, it sets the

---

1. Projects@Work, "Poor Communication Top Cause of Project Failure," March 14, 2007, www.projectsatwork.com/content/articles/235492.cfm.

tone for everything that follows. If the briefing is rushed or sloppy, guess what? The mission will be rushed and sloppy! But if the briefing is crisp, detailed, and well coordinated, that's how the mission will go.

Do you and your wingmen brief a plan to succeed when launching a project, tackling a sale, planning a meeting, or opening a new store? Have you created an easily understood "lost comm" procedure to handle potential problems? And, most important, do you have full buy-in to the plan—are your wingmen committed to the mission's success?

CHECK-IN

Throughout a mission, fighter pilots have planned times, when they not only check each other in on the radio to ensure that every wingman is on the correct frequency but also share information about their fuel state, the status of weapons systems, and any irregularity that may have come up. These pre-established check-in points ensure that everyone is heading in the "same way, same day." If something irregular or nonstandard is shared, the team can troubleshoot immediately and adapt the plan accordingly.

For example, if a wingman is having an engine problem or a fuel tank isn't feeding, another wingman will rejoin on their wing and help run through various checklists to get the problem fixed as soon as possible. This concept of mutual support is critical in times of emergency, because when trying to fix a problem, a pilot may fail to cross-check his altitude, attitude, or heading and get off course. When trying to fix a problem, it's easy to bury your head in the cockpit and let the aircraft point toward the ground. Your wingmen will keep you straight and level.

But checking in does more than solve problems during an emergency. It provides valuable information about people's attitudes and the current environment in the workplace, and, most important, it lets people know they are valued and appreciated. Leaders need to have high situational awareness of their people.

BE A "PSYCHO"

I remember accidentally sleeping in one morning and being late for a mission briefing at the 559th Flying Training Squadron in San Antonio, Texas, where I was an instructor pilot. When you're late for a briefing, there are always consequences. First, you are grounded for the day (meaning you can't fly). Second, you have to bring doughnuts for the pilots. So I picked up some Krispy Kreme doughnuts, dropped them off to my wingmen, apologized for being late, and then reluctantly sat down at my desk to get some paperwork done. Fifteen minutes later, the briefing room door burst open and out piled eight excited pilots who were ready to fly. The last person out of the room was my flight commander, Maj. Pat White. Quiet, unassuming, and intense, he was no ordinary commander. The call sign he earned in my squadron said it all: "Psycho." Seeing him walk toward me, I took a deep breath and prepared to get chewed out.

"Hey, Waldo, how's it going?" he asked.

"I'm doing fine, Psycho. Sorry for being late. It won't happen again."

"That's OK, Waldo. Listen, this isn't like you. You're never late. Is everything OK at home? Are you feeling all right? Do you need a day off? Talk to me."

I was stunned. "Seriously, Psycho," I said, "I'm doing fine. I just messed up setting my alarm. Stupid mistake. Everything at home is great. Just give me a doughnut and I'll be on my way." I tried not to look uneasy.

"All right, Waldo. But just let me know if I can help you with anything." He smiled and walked away, never mentioning anything about it again.

His comments were totally unexpected, and I remember actually feeling pretty good when he walked away. Instead of reprimanding me, Psycho made me feel valued. He acknowledged me as a person first, and as a pilot second. He taught me a lesson in the value of the check-in for building situational awareness.

Psycho showed me he was a great communicator and caring leader *by the questions he asked.* And then he sat back patiently and listened.

Colin Powell had it right when he said, "Leadership is solving problems. The day soldiers stop bringing you their problems is the day they have lost confidence that you can help or concluded that you don't care."

Because Psycho cared, I felt an even deeper loyalty to him. I volunteered for the tough jobs (without feeling resentful), brought the problems I couldn't solve to him, spent extra time at work when needed, and got my head in the books. My commitment to Psycho, and ultimately the mission, went up. I became a better instructor pilot and officer. Mind you, Psycho treated everyone with respect, and it made me realize that was the reason he was chosen to be a flight commander.

Attitude is contagious and so is performance. Everyone worked harder for Psycho, and this resulted in a superior squadron of committed wingmen. Great communication improves morale and builds trust, both of which lead to higher-performing individuals and teams. And in an organization that lives or dies by performance, morale and trust are priceless.

ASK THE RIGHT QUESTIONS

What questions are you asking your coworkers, customers, and wingmen to show them that you value them? Are you letting them cross the border on their own and in the dark? Or are you listening to what they say and checking them in to make sure they're on frequency?

The bottom line is that *people are far more effective when they understand and feel understood.* That means maintaining face-to-face or voice contact with your wingmen. It means understanding their challenges, listening to their issues, and, most importantly, *asking the right questions.* Checking in to make sure your wingmen are on frequency and keeping open communication with your team minimizes the stress of change and adversity and creates a performance-enhancing environment of trust.

PICK UP THE PHONE

A few years back, while speaking at a national sales meeting for a large medical device company, I asked the number one salesperson for the key to his success. "That's easy, Waldo," he replied. "I pick up the phone."

I loved this answer. He began to rant and rave about how too many salespeople rely on e-mails alone to communicate with their clients. He said he spends most of his time calling his clients and connecting with them. Sure, it takes more time, but they appreciate it, and his sales figures show it.

With today's e-mails, autoresponders, social networking sites, and BlackBerries, it's easy to forget the basics of communication. But never forget that *people like to be treated as human beings first and businesspeople second.* For many of us, calling is a simply a luxury we *think* we can't afford in the moment. But when you go the extra mile and pick up the phone, you strengthen your relationships and distinguish yourself from the average businessperson. This can make a huge difference, not only in your business but in your personal life.

Here are some simple but effective steps you can take to practice solid, *personal* communication with the people who count:

• Although e-mail is an effective time-saving tool, use it judiciously. And when it comes to sensitive issues, be aware that because e-mail can't convey subtle vocal nuances, it can often be misinterpreted. When in doubt about how the recipient might read your message, pick up the phone instead. *A one-minute phone call can accomplish more than ten e-mails.*

• Remember, it's not what you say that matters; it's what is heard. When confronted with a challenge, think of a unique way to communicate with your client or associate. Realize the impact your words and tone may have on the receiver.

• Stay personal. Don't forget to keep in touch with your friends, customers, and family members. They are your wingmen, too. Make it a point to call or send a handwritten note or card to those in your life whom you truly care about. Take them to lunch. Appreciate them. Do a small act of kindness that says to the other person, "You matter to me." How do *you* feel when you haven't heard from a friend in a month or two?

GET EVERYONE ON THE SAME FREQUENCY

What if my flight lead had failed to check me in on our mission in Iraq? With no radio communication, I would have been kept in the dark and would have had a really tough time making it back to base. Average teams *assume* that everyone is on the same frequency. Great teams (and great wingmen) check in with each other to *make sure of it.* They reach out and never leave each other in the dark.

Are you checking in with your wingmen—your vendors, suppliers, sales reps, and friends—when you have not heard from them for a while, or do you just assume that everything's OK? Maybe they're in the dark and screaming for help but just don't have the means or courage to ask for it. Even worse, they may not feel they have any wingmen to go to for help.

Have you ever felt isolated and stressed out while dealing with a problem but then got a phone call from a friend at just the right time? That's what good wingmen do. They keep in touch. They reach out. They acknowledge each other. They check in to make sure their wingmen aren't flying blind and are on frequency. Lose sight, lose fight.

Leaving even one of your wingmen in the dark, with no situational awareness, guarantees one certainty: you will have second-guessers making decisions on their own that might not be in the best interests of the mission and the rest of the team.

Finally, if you are tumbleweed or losing situational awareness, fess up early. The biggest problems develop when a wingman fails to disclose a problem early and tries to solve it on his or her own. The situation snowballs, and what could have been solved with a simple correction turns into a bigger situation that affects the entire mission.

DEBRIEF TO BUILD SITUATIONAL AWARENESS

It doesn't help to wallow in the past, but you can certainly debrief and learn from your mistakes. And if you do, you'll find that having a good comm plan and "radio-out" procedures will keep you off tumbleweed status and help you avoid some very nasty situations.

Ask the managers at JetBlue. Following a devastating blizzard in the Northeast in the winter of 2007, the airline faced thousands of customer complaints and paid out millions of dollars after a series of bad communication incidents left passengers trapped in planes on the runway for up to ten and a half hours. The company later explained that a series of communication snafus between JetBlue and airport authorities had forced the airline to keep passengers on the planes despite their being parked right next to the terminal.

If the airline had decided to cancel flights earlier and had a predetermined communication plan among JetBlue ground personnel, flight crews, and airport authorities—not to mention with the National Weather Service—the results would have been a lot more pleasant for all involved.

What happened after JetBlue management sat down and debriefed? The airline vowed to communicate in a more consistent, timely fashion with all parties, especially with custom-ers.[2] Following the blizzard fiasco, customers lost trust in JetBlue, and the airline's stock plummeted. Trust is easy to lose but hard to regain—and communication is the linchpin.

LEADING THE WAY

Leadership has nothing to do with rank or position. It's about action, respect, and influence. Regardless of your position, be the one to lead the way with communication standards.

The following additional action steps will help catapult your communications efforts:

• **Have a mass briefing at least once a month.** Gather your wingmen and communicate the latest trends, organiza-tional goals, safety updates, customer initiatives, and any other important developments. Keep everyone in the know, not in the dark. Your wingmen need to hear important news—good or bad—from you first.

• **Conduct feedback sessions on a consistent basis.** Many leaders conduct an "out briefing" with employees or vendors they are letting go. Leadership consultant Kristi Petersen sug-gests conducting a "stay briefing." Sit down with your coworkers, vendors, and partners and let them know how they are doing. Are they meeting your expectations? If not, let them know as soon as possible. Be detailed, devise an action plan, and set a timeline for results. Ask your wingmen about

---

2. Patrick J. Lyons, "A Snowshocked JetBlue Hits the Cancel Button," *The Lede*, March 16, 2007, http://thelede.blogs.nytimes.com/2007/03/16/a-snowshocked-jet -blue-hits-the-cancel-button.

their goals and what kind of challenges they are facing. Take time to solicit feedback on *yourself* as a leader, coworker, or peer. What would they like to see from you? Do the same with your customers. Look for bottlenecks to productivity or customer service challenges, and solicit your wingmen's suggestions on how to handle them.

• **Walk the flight line.** Get your hands dirty with your wingmen. Spend time with them on the job and observe how they do business. Ask questions about their work challenges and their personal lives. Show them you care. We'll discuss this in detail in Chapter 10.

• **Debrief your missions.** After every critical mission, conduct a blameless, rankless debrief. Find out if objectives were met, and analyze why they weren't. Search for trends and communicate these to the rest of your organization. Lessons learned should not be kept solely within your squadron. Share them openly with your other wingmen.

The seeds of trust are planted with communication, sown through action, and nurtured with understanding. Going out of your way to connect with your wingmen will result in trusting, successful relationships that maintain situational awareness when the skies are dark and the missiles are launched. Don't leave interpersonal connections out of your flight plan.

WALDO'S WINGTIP

"Knock it off" is the statement wingmen call out to each other when safety is violated on a training sortie or when an emergency occurs. All wingmen in the formation discontinue their current maneuver and get to a safe distance from other aircraft while climbing to a safe altitude. Then the situation can be analyzed safely and effectively. When communication is minimal or you find yourself with little or no situational awareness, be willing to put your ego aside and call a "knock it off" to your team. Share your challenge and work to get everyone heading the same way before continuing the mission. This also applies to you as a leader. You may see an unsafe situation or a confrontation brewing that warrants a "knock it off." Better to call it early and err on the side of being overly cautious rather than delay and exert far more time and energy dealing with the negative ramifications.

9

Abort! Abort!

The Courage to Quit

I'M EXHAUSTED BUT can't sleep. It's a chilly sixty-five degrees in the hotel room, but I'm sweating profusely. My mind won't stop racing.

In just a few hours I'll be strapping into an F-16 for an eight-hour nonstop flight home from Morón Air Base in Spain to Shaw Air Force Base in South Carolina. This is not a combat mission. There will be no missiles and no night refueling in thunderstorms—just a mellow cross-country flight to the good old United States.

There's only one problem. It's called the Atlantic Ocean. Thirty-five hundred miles of nothing but me, my F-16, and freezing-cold water. What did I get myself into?

Like a fool, I volunteered to be one of the six fighter pilots in my squadron to ferry an F-16 back to our home base at Shaw. We had just completed a two-month deployment to Saudi Arabia, flying combat missions in southern Iraq to enforce the no-fly zone. When the commander asked for volunteers to fly back, I raised my hand.

I can do this, I thought to myself. After all, I had survived six-hour night combat missions in Iraq and Kosovo. How bad could it be? It would be a challenge, sure, but also fun.

I was conveniently forgetting about my claustrophobia.

So here I am, at three A.M., wondering if I'll have a panic attack at twenty thousand feet and fifteen hundred miles out to sea. Will I be able to control myself as I did in the past on those harrowing combat missions? Or will I lose focus and spiral into a fit of hysteria and panic, alone and strapped tightly inside a coffinlike cockpit, with the nearest emergency airfield more than two hours away? My head spins as I ponder every possible emergency procedure. I don't sleep a wink.

I stumble out of bed at seven A.M., exhausted, and barely eat breakfast. Anxious and miserable, I have a pounding headache during the premission brief, reminding me of how little sleep I've had. I can't shake my anxiety and ponder asking the commander to replace me with another pilot. I talk myself out of it. There is no way I am going to wimp out and embarrass myself in front of my wingmen. I'm tougher than that. I'm no coward.

Besides, I can't tell anyone the reason *why* I'm so stressed, why I couldn't sleep last night. If I do, they'll rip the Air Force wings off my chest so fast, I won't have time to think. I hid my little secret for seven years, and there's no way I'm going to tell anyone about it now. I'll fly the mission and live up to my commitment. I'm a fighter pilot, for goodness sake!

I strap on my survival gear, grab my helmet bag, and head out to the jet with my five wingmen. It's gorgeous out, and a slight breeze cools the air. Soon we'll be home with our families, enjoying a home-cooked meal and our own warm beds. No more living in tents, eating powdered eggs and Saudi desert sand. No more night missions trying to refuel on a tanker while fighting vertigo.

I try to get jazzed, but I can't. With each step toward the aircraft, my anxiety grows along with my fear.

I climb into the cockpit, run through the preflight checklist, and hear the commander give us the start-engines call. Here we go. I take a deep breath and get ready to crank up the massive F-16 General Electric engine. It's go time.

What the heck am I *doing*? Do I *really* need to fly this jet today? Is flying home *that* mission-critical? Are we at war here?

If I take off in this plane, I cannot say with 100 percent certainty that I won't freak out and have a panic attack. And if I do, then I'll become a serious safety hazard, not only to myself but to my wingmen as well. Is it really worth that risk?

I have to make a critical decision and make it quick. *Fly or abort?*

My crew chief looks up at me, waiting for the start-engine signal.

I can't do this. Damn it!

I call out to my flight lead, Lieutenant Colonel Dodson, who is also our squadron commander—my boss, "One, this is Two."

"Go ahead."

"Uh, yeah. Uh . . . Two needs to abort."

There's a slight pause. "Say again?"

"Two's aborting, sir."

Another pregnant pause follows. "State reason."

"Yes, sir. Uh . . . I am feeling, uh, pretty sick. Not sure I can make it all the way home. I didn't sleep last night and feel like crap."

If I could hear the comments coming from the other pilots, I'm sure their words would sting. Aborting this flight will alter the entire flight plan. Everyone will be affected: the tanker and maintenance crews, the air traffic controllers, and the pilots. My wingmen will need to sit on the ground for at least another hour, get a replacement pilot briefed and into my jet, and adjust the clearance. We were on our way home, and now, because of me, the mission will be delayed, maybe even scrapped until tomorrow.

An eternity seems to pass before the radio lights up again.

"OK, guys, shut 'em down and meet at Base Operations in ten minutes."

I walk back to Base Operations nauseated, embarrassed, and ready to get railed at by my wingmen. I imagine what they'll say: "What the heck, Waldo? I can't believe you just aborted!" "What's your problem? Couldn't you just suck this one up for the team?" I beat myself up.

Back in Base Operations, I explain to my wingmen that I barely slept last night, had a pounding headache, and felt exhausted. I couldn't risk falling asleep while heading home. "I'm sorry, guys, I just couldn't do it." Sure, all this is true. But I don't tell them (nor do I need to) that the reason I couldn't sleep was because of my anxiety and my secret fear of having a claustrophobic panic attack over the Atlantic Ocean!

I wait for their verbal lashing, but to my utter surprise, it never comes. They're totally cool about it. While they are disappointed about the delay, nobody doubts my judgment, questions my credibility, or sees me as a "loser." They don't beat me up the way I imagined they would.

Within minutes, another pilot who was set to fly home the following day—sitting sideways in a cargo plane—gladly volunteers to take my spot. He's more than happy to change places with me because it means he'll be home a whole day earlier—and he won't have to sit sideways for thirty-five hundred miles. My decision to abort, it turns out, delays the mission by only one hour, and the ferry flight home to Shaw winds up being a success.

That night, I pondered my decision to abort the mission. At first, I thought of myself as a total failure. I felt ashamed in some strange way. I was disappointed that I gave in to my fear for the first time in my career. *What is wrong with me?* I thought. *How could I be so weak?*

I called my twin brother, Dave, and my parents. I had to get this off my chest. "Did I do the right thing, guys? Did I mess up?" They were very supportive and helped me see the benefit of my decision. After a few days of deep reflection and feedback from some of my trusted friends, I finally realized I had made the right decision.

The lessons I learned that day changed the way I look at quitting, for the rest of my life.

MAKING A GO/NO-GO DECISION

Through sixty-five combat missions and eleven years of intensive Air Force flying, that flight from Spain to the United States was the only one I ever aborted out of fear. I should be proud of that fact, but for years I thought I was a failure because I quit that day. It has taken me a lot of self-reflection and life experience to finally understand that there *is* a time and a place to quit, and quit honorably. It's what I want to share with you in this chapter. But first I want to share with you reasons why you *shouldn't* quit.

You may be wondering how I was able to fly so many combat missions as a claustrophobic and never abort. How can this relate to you when you're faced with a decision to press on or quit?

Before deciding to quit a mission, you have to ask yourself three questions:

- *Why* am I on this mission?
- What are the *consequences*, and will others be negatively affected if I abort this mission?
- If I abort, will I be shirking my assigned *responsibilities* and *commitments*?

In May 1990, at my graduation from the Air Force Academy, I raised my right hand that proudly displayed my academy ring, and took the oath of office for the United States Air Force. It was a firm and public commitment that I would "well and faithfully discharge the duties of the office upon which I am about to enter." I then spent the next several years earning my pilot wings, serving as an instructor pilot, and then flying operationally in the F-16.

I was, and still am, an officer in the United States Air Force. I have a duty to fulfill and a commitment to live up to. In combat, I had a duty to serve the people who needed me to help restore peace in the face of adversity. Moreover, my wingmen also needed me to stick it through and push it up, because without me the entire mission would suffer. They needed the mutual support that I could provide.

What would my academy ring and years of military training mean if I didn't have the courage to step up and fly in real combat, when it really mattered? What would *your* education, professional training, and character mean if you quit every time things got tough?

As professionals, we need to step up and have the character and strength to *do the right thing* even though it may be challenging and painful. As executives, entrepreneurs, managers, coaches, parents, and friends, we have to live up to our commitments and responsibilities to fulfill the roles we signed up for. We can't just abort at the first sign of struggle. Imagine if all our soldiers turned tail and ran when they first saw the enemy.

Today we see too much of exactly that behavior. It's what erodes the fabric of the business world and the society we live in. We watch with resentment as executives embezzle money from their employees and shareholders. We watch in horror as our own politicians sell out to greed and participate in shady negotiations. We see managers make false promises to clients on deliverables and fees, eroding the reputation of their companies. And we see married couples with children divorce when their relationship is tested, without really trying to work things out.

So why does this occur?

Fear. Fear of failure. Fear of mediocrity. Fear of not being accepted or liked. Fear even of success. The list goes on.

We have to live up to a higher standard and not forsake our values, our purpose, and our wingmen at the first sign of adversity. This is what reaching new heights is all about.

But it's not always easy. We need to focus on those things that are *greater than our fears* if we hope to muster the courage to strap in, take off, and face the missiles.

What gave me the courage not to quit was my commitment to live up to my obligation as an officer, not leave my wingmen hanging, and, finally, to serve those who needed help. But it was also my fear of being thought a coward by my wingmen that pushed me to strap in and fly. My fear of shame and being seen as weak actually eclipsed my fear of having a panic attack!

In business, project managers often push through projects when they know they should abort, for fear of being rebuked by their bosses. New sales reps are afraid to raise their hand at company meetings for verification on policies or procedures, for fear that others will think they are incompetent. Regional sales reps keep spending time on unproductive legacy accounts. The list of examples goes on and on.

I share this with you now because my courage builders were not present when I strapped into the F-16 at Morón Air Base in Spain. Because I couldn't find something to focus on that was greater than my fear of claustrophobia, I aborted. I couldn't find meaning in my mission. I didn't have a higher calling. There weren't people to save. My wingmen didn't absolutely *need* me to fly that day. It was not combat. I didn't *have* to fly.

The only thing at stake was my ego. I was too afraid of looking like a wimp and embarrassing myself to do the right thing and abort—right up until the start-engine signal. Have you ever been guilty of that? Our egos can truly impair our judgment and force us to do things we know we shouldn't.

Egos incite fear. *Fear unfaced leads to doubt. Doubt is what robs us of our warrior spirit.*

Instead of hanging on to that mission and flying for the wrong reasons—to save face—I realized that by aborting, I was doing myself and my wingmen a huge favor. By not acting out of false bravado and pretending to be a hero, I avoided a potentially serious safety incident. I had to come to grips with the need to *abort the ego*, which ultimately causes more lapses in judgment than just about anything else in business and in life.

Most important, what I learned from this experience is that it's normal to be scared. It's part of what makes us human. We can't be fearless superheroes all the time and fly *every* mission.

So, I challenge you to reflect deeply on your purpose and on who needs you. Also, think about the consequences if you should quit. *Find out what gives meaning to your mission*, and you will be able to gather the strength and courage to press on despite your fears. And finally, get out of your head and abort your ego—you'll be able to make a much more informed and qualified decision about whether to take off or abort.

WINGMEN HELP US BAIL OUT WHEN WE NEED TO ABORT

On every mission, fighter pilots are briefed with a go/no-go decision that details our abort criteria. This is the point at which we must decide: continue to the target, or abort? If we abort, we turn around as fast as possible and regroup or wait to fly another day. But once past the go/no-go point, we are committed to the target.

In March 2000, a good friend of mine, "Moose," was performing at an air show in Texas. Tremendously experienced, he was the West Coast F-16 demo pilot and flew dozens of special solo performances every year. One windy day in Texas, Moose misjudged his altitude at the top of a split-S maneuver, and while upside down and pulling through the maneuver, he passed his go/no-go point and crashed. He left behind a wife and two children.

The fighter pilot community was shocked and deeply saddened by this loss. How could such an experienced pilot have made such a mistake? What went wrong? Dozens of factors could have played a part in the accident. Perhaps he was cross-checking his airspeed more than his altitude. Or maybe he was worrying about his alignment with the runway. Perhaps his situational awareness had dropped due to some minor systems malfunction.

Unfortunately, Moose was flying solo. He didn't have an in-flight wingman to check his six and tell him to cross-check his altitude or airspeed. No one was there to radio "Bail out!" in time. Had there been, perhaps he would still be with us.

As I mentioned in Chapter 3, we all have our blind spots. When we're focused on the task at hand, blind spots develop, and we may not see the big picture. We may even be "tumbleweed," flying along thinking everything is perfect. We may not see the ground coming or even realize we're close to crashing. In those cases, we need our wingmen to help build our situational awareness by calling out "Break right!" And if necessary, we may need them to tell us to bail out.

As wingmen, we owe it to our team of partners to make the bail-out call if we see they need it. Perhaps we need to end a long project draining us of critical resources. Or we may need to change jobs and find work that has more meaning for us. Perhaps that little "personal habit" we have is a lot worse than we realize. We have to think outside the cockpit and extend mutual support to others in our lives. And most important, we need to be willing to call out for help.

Will you have the awareness and the courage to put your ego aside and bring your problems and challenges to a wingman on a tough initiative, project, or personal issue? Will you solicit feedback from those who will challenge you and tell you straight up what you *need* to hear and not from yes-men who tell you what you *want* to hear? Are you willing to expose your weaknesses, doubts, and fears and solicit your wingmen's thoughts and opinions? And having asked, will you listen to them and take the appropriate action? Perhaps they will tell you to bail out and quit. Or they may encourage you to stick with the mission, because you may not see the impact your abort will have on your wingmen or those you love.

Unlike Moose, that morning at Morón I had wingmen I could call out to for help, but my ego stopped me. Even though I had wingmen, I thought and acted as if I were taking off from Spain on a solo mission. And because of that, I thought I messed up when I decided to quit.

Jet fighters have ejection seats because no aircraft is perfect. Neither is the pilot—and neither are you. You'll make mistakes. You may need to use that ejection seat because you may not see the missile hurtling toward your aircraft or because you realize you're on the wrong flight path. My advice to you is to quit with confidence. But quit only after you've *earned the right* to quit. And after you quit, dust yourself off, find a mission worth flying, and then get back to work planning for that new mission.

Ultimately, you alone can make the final decision. But don't make that decision solo. When you have a wingman or two who care about you and are really looking out for your best interest, making that call will be a lot easier. Fortunately for me, I learned this lesson on a mission I never flew. Sometimes it's better to stay on the ground than fly with a broken wing.

WALDO'S WINGTIP

Start a "Buddy Wingman" Program at Work

When new pilots show up to a squadron, they are assigned a buddy. This buddy is an experienced pilot who shows them the ropes and gives guidance and perspective when needed. The new pilot comes to this wingman with his or her problems and questions, and the buddy makes it a priority to see that they are handled. The buddy also supports the new pilot in not quitting when things get rough.

When a new employee shows up at your office, assign a buddy wingman to the new hire to facilitate the in-processing and get him or her up to speed. The new hire won't feel alone and left behind in the bustle of the workplace. And when the new hire feels overwhelmed and like quitting, he or she will have a wingman to go to who has his or her back. Not only will this improve morale and productivity, but it will also reduce turnover.

10

Walk the Flight Line

Connecting with Your Wingmen

IT'S RARE FOR the squadron commander to meet you at your jet after a training mission. So when I saw Lieutenant Colonel Dodson approaching my F-16 with a stern look on his face, I knew something was up.

"Waldo, we need to talk," he said as I climbed down the ladder from the cockpit and jumped onto the tarmac.

"Yes, sir," I replied, and waited, a little uneasily, for what was coming next. Had I messed up? Was I in trouble? I gulped. Was something wrong at home?

"Waldo, Airman Tyler told me what happened before you took off this afternoon, and I am not impressed." His tone was serious, and I instantly knew what he was referring to.

Just three hours earlier, during my after-engine-start checklist, I had noticed that my jet was shorted five hundred pounds of fuel. Not a huge amount but enough to cut my rare and treasured air-to-air training mission by at least ten minutes (an eternity to a fighter pilot). Although atypical, sometimes the wing tanks just won't fill up completely, and there is nothing the crew chief responsible for fueling the jet can do about it. I was frustrated because my training was going to be cut short, and instead of sucking it up, I got steamed and insulted the young crew chief, Airman Tyler, for being complacent. I blamed him for the tanks not being full. My sharp remarks stung. They were also unnecessary.

"Waldo, do you realize how hard our crew chiefs work just so we have mission-ready jets to fly?" It was pretty clear that my commander wasn't pleased. "Do you know how many hours they spend on the flight line?"

I was at a loss for words. I had messed up, and there was no excuse.

The colonel continued, "Waldo, I'm taking you off the flying schedule tomorrow. Dig out your oldest flight suit and report to the maintenance hangar at six A.M. You're going spend the day on the flight line with the troops." I saluted smartly and headed to my debriefing.

The next day was one of the longest in my eleven years of active duty in the Air Force. I was up at the crack of dawn and spent the day fueling jets, inspecting engines, moving fifty-five-gallon drums full of used oil, and running inventory on aircraft parts.

By the end of the day, I was done in. My hands were caked with grease, I smelled as if I'd been dipped in jet fuel, and my flight suit was trashed with a huge black oil streak down the length of each pant leg. I still have that flight suit today to remind me how my words and actions affect others.

And yet, while the labor was grueling, the experience was immensely rewarding. It gave me the opportunity to walk in the shoes of some wingmen vital to the mission of the 79th Fighter Squadron. I listened to their complaints, empathized with their frustrations, and got a much better feel for all the things they did to make the mission happen. Basically, I was one of the guys for a day, and there was no rank or position separating us. And despite all I knew about what maintenance did to support the pilots, the experience painted a clear picture of what *really* went into giving me a jet that was "MR"—mission-ready.

The crew chiefs were the ones prepping the jets to fly. They performed the detailed inspections and exhausting labor behind the scenes to make sure the F-16s were safe to fly. They checked the engines and made sure the oil was clean, the tires were inflated, and the weapons systems worked properly. Without them, the mission wouldn't happen.

Most were just out of high school and barely twenty years old. Some even had dreams of becoming fighter pilots but didn't have the parental guidance, the grades, or the money to go to college or the eyesight to fly. Many were actually in college, getting their degrees, with the hope of becoming officers one day. They looked up to and respected the pilots of the 79th. I lost that respect from Airman Tyler. One thing was certain: he no longer looked at me as a wingman. I was not his trusted partner. I became a wing nut.

While working with the troops, I realized that we had more in common than I had thought. Like me, those crew chiefs had families and friends back home, whom they missed. They, too, had to deploy to remote, desolate locations such as Saudi Arabia, sleep in tents, eat lousy food, and make that same chilly predawn hundred-yard walk to the showers. They, too, had demanding supervisors, who pushed them to perform and expected nothing less than excellence.

Before this humbling experience, I was pretty much blind to the behind-the-scenes maintenance wingmen of my squadron. Although I thought I knew their job responsibilities, I didn't appreciate the sacrifices they made for the mission. I really didn't consider them my wingmen.

A day on the flight line changed my perspective forever.

WHO'S ON YOUR FLIGHT LINE?

Are *you* getting out there with your wingmen and walking the flight line? Do you know their issues, gripes, and personal concerns? Do you appreciate the sacrifices they make in accomplishing the mission at work? And do you know what gets in the way of their giving their best? In short, have you connected with your wingmen?

Every day you have the opportunity to get to know your wingmen on a deeper level. Are you taking advantage of those opportunities? When is the last time you took a few minutes out of your daily routine to "walk the flight line"?

A few years back, I conducted a leadership keynote address at an annual meeting for the Federal Judiciary Council in Washington, D.C. As part of my premission preparation, I decided to visit the federal branch offices for Georgia in downtown Atlanta. After our pre-mission briefing with his senior staff, Federal Clerk James Hatten (a retired Army colonel and a West Point graduate) took me on a tour of his office. What happened next really made me think a little bit differently about leadership.

We walked through every office and cubicle (about twenty of them), and Jim personally introduced me to his entire staff. He called them by their first names, knew how long they had been with the organization, what their current projects were, and even the names of their children and spouses. When he approached them, they smiled, and their eyes lit up. They liked Jim because they knew he genuinely cared about them.

When I asked Jim how he managed to memorize all that personal information, he simply said that his job was to *serve his staff.* If he was not committed to serving them and acknowledging them for all they did, then how could he expect them to sacrifice, put in the long hours, and go the extra mile for him? It was obvious he knew a thing or two about leadership.

A true leader is a servant. To lead, you need to have influence. To have influence, you must command respect, and you gain it through your actions, your commitment, and your integrity. These are the fundamentals of establishing wingman relationships.

How your wingmen perceive you is just as important as your philosophy. What you say, how you dress, and how you treat others is being judged all day, every day. It doesn't end when you leave work.

I didn't show respect for Airman Tyler through my actions. He had done his best to serve me and the other men and women of the 79th, but I didn't show him that I valued him. I didn't serve him or appreciate him. In this respect, I failed to check Airman Tyler's six. Guess what happens when people don't feel that their six is being checked? They check out. I couldn't afford to have Airman Tyler, or *any* of my crew chiefs, check out. After all, they had my life in their hands. If they became complacent while inspecting my jet and missed a critical safety item, I could be in trouble.

In business, if you don't check your wingmen's six, your wingmen may check out. They may get complacent. If this happens, then they won't go the extra mile to double-check the accuracy of their work, provide above and beyond customer service, put in the hours necessary to make sure a project gets done right, or give a top gun presentation to a client. In highly competitive work environments that are constantly changing, you can't afford to have your team check out. Everyone, regardless of their role, contributes to a mission's overall success. So always respect and appreciate your wingmen. Put in the effort to check their blind spots. Call out the missiles, and give feedback when necessary. Offer your help, and say "thank you" whenever you can. By doing this, you'll build a trustworthy and committed team that will drive you and your whole organization to new heights.

GET YOUR WINGMEN IN FORMATION

Jim Collins is the author of the bestselling book *Good to Great*, one of the best business leadership books ever written. In *Good to Great*, Collins uses the analogy of *getting the right people on the right bus* before executing a business strategy. While this makes sense conceptually, I prefer to look at the bus analogy in a different way.

Have you ever been on a private or public bus? Can you remember, back in high school, taking a field trip to the museum or to a special event? What were the passengers doing in the back of the bus? Reading, sleeping, listening to music, maybe even misbehaving. In essence, they were doing nothing! The only person doing anything to get the bus where it needed to go was the driver.

That's fine for a field trip, but it's no way to run a business. When you gather a team of wingmen to accomplish a mission, they need to get on board and get to work! They shouldn't be sitting around doing nothing and shooting the breeze while you lead them to the target. Leaders don't loaf, and neither do their teams.

In the fighter pilot world, we have formations that are composed of several jets. Each formation has a flight lead responsible for leading the mission, but all the jets are manned by fully accountable and focused fighter pilots with specific roles to fulfill. These wingmen work as a team to get the job done, and if one fails to do his or her job, the whole mission is apt to fail.

But the team doesn't stop there—maintenance crews, intelligence officers, tanker pilots, weather forecasters, and many others are also part of the formation. Guess what happens to the mission if they don't do their job?

The problem in business today is that many employees *act* as if they were on a bus. They essentially say, "Hey, [manager, VP, or CEO], here I am, ready for you to lead me to the target. I'll be right here, just sitting in the back of the bus and relaxing." Or they *feel* as if they were on a bus because the leader doesn't bother to connect with them, assign them responsibilities, and appreciate them.

In the corporate world, people may have well-paying positions and be highly skilled, but if they haven't emotionally bought into a mission or the leader, then sooner or later they will become apathetic and make mistakes. They'll just be relaxing in the back of the bus.

If your wingmen don't care whether your company or your shared endeavor survives in this tough economy, they won't go above and beyond when you need them to.

Conversely, if your wingmen feel served and respected by you, they *will* put up with the extra work, cost-cutting, and all the less-than-desirable aspects of the typical workplace.

So are *you* treating your wingmen like members of a formation, or like students on a field trip bus? Are you spending some time with your IT staff to see what their day actually looks like—the hoops they have to jump through to make sure your website, computers, and software are up to speed? Do you walk the factory floor and talk to the quality assurance inspector about the challenges she may be facing? Have you ever spent a day with your channel partners and joined them on a few sales calls? Think of the effect that would have.

William James, the great nineteenth-century psychologist, said that the *desire to be appreciated* is one of the deepest drives in human nature. One study of a number of large corporations revealed that the number one reason people quit their jobs was, as they put it, "No one appreciated what I did."

Knowing that our contribution is valued gives us fuel to crank our engines to afterburner when the heat is on and trouble comes zinging our way. It gives us power to thrust forward through change, failure, or rejection.

Remember, you don't have to be a supervisor or a C-level corporate officer to walk the flight line. Anyone can do it. You just have to extend a hand and connect with people one-on-one.

FLIGHT LINE CHECKLIST

The following is a checklist to help you create the habit of walking your flight line. These activities should be part of your routine whether or not you're in a formal leadership role.

- Determine the ten people you work with who most directly influence the outcomes of your job. This is your flight line.

- Whenever possible, you should share a meal with someone. Each week, take one person out to breakfast or lunch from a department other than your own. It's a good way to connect informally, and it will allow both of you to open up and see each other as people, not just coworkers.
- Schedule a (unannounced) "squadron tour." Visit your various "shops," and randomly, in a way that doesn't put anyone on the spot, interview your wingmen. Ask what their biggest challenges are and how you can help them.
- Sit in on a strategy session with your marketing team, or a weekly budget update with a project manager. Share best practices with these groups. Ask for suggestions. Step outside your silo.

If I had done some of these things a lot more when I was in the Air Force, perhaps I would have been able to connect more with Airman Tyler and would not have been so condescending. Naturally, we all have our bad days. We're going to say things and act in ways that rub people the wrong way. As a New Yorker, believe me, I do that. But sometimes the best thing to do is to say the words that are absolutely essential to building and maintaining a wingman relationship. Those words are "I'm sorry."

Apologizing won't necessarily fix the problem or gain back someone's favor, but it's a start at mending a relationship, and it can do wonders for mending your reputation as well.

Right about now you may be saying, "Look, Waldo, my wingmen already know me, and I know them. They know I care." Well, that may be so, but it's important to connect continuously and not take any relationship for granted (especially with all the job turnover that goes on today). Relationships need continual nurturing and reconnection. This holds true for your best employees as well as your top customers. The last thing you want is your best customer checking out because you haven't stayed in touch. Remember, "lose sight, lose fight." You have to walk the flight line of your customers as well. It's an ongoing investment. If you are not staying connected, you'll never know when there's a missile launch— a family tragedy, a personal challenge, a supplier issue, or a quality-control problem—or when there is a big win to celebrate.

Remember, relationships are about *relating*. If you don't spend time relating with your team, there *won't be* any relationship.

A few years back, I was stationed at Kunsan Air Base in South Korea with the mighty 35th Fighter Squadron "Pantons." My squadron commander, Lt. Col. Mike Johnson, unexpectedly came by my apartment one night to review my officer performance report, fix some errors, and generally help me to sharpen it. It was a Friday night, and he could have been at a bar with some of the guys or on the phone with his wife and kids in the States. But instead, he took the time to attend to me and my career because he knew how important it was. He went above and beyond and, in the process, earned my respect—and, most important, my loyalty. You can bet that when he needed a volunteer to tackle some menial job that no one wanted to do, I would raise my hand.

When it comes to trust, developing "wingmanship" has a cumulative effect. It grows like a snowball rolling down a hill.

But if you don't nurture it, the snow will melt and you'll have to start all over again. And believe me when I say it takes a lot more time and effort to start a relationship all over than to nurture what you already have.

A caveat here: be careful not to nurture out of personal need. When you truly serve, it's always about the other person. If all you do is walk the flight line with people who are only going to get you business or help you in your career, you're missing the concept. We all know of master networkers who are schmoozing all the time, "building relationships" only because it will get them business. They see a prospect with a big dollar sign on her forehead, and suddenly they're best friends. But it's phony caring, and sooner or later the "friend" gets recognized for what he is: a user.

Be the wingman who donates time and coaches peers and doesn't expect anything. I truly believe that the profound blessings I have had as a professional leadership speaker and consultant are a direct result of the people I've helped. Not because they returned the favor, but because there are dozens of wingmen who have gone way above and beyond for *me*. I acknowledge those who have helped me, by doing the best job I can of staying in touch and letting them know I genuinely appreciate them for the impact they have had on my life. I refer them business when I can, send them gifts, and offer testimonials. How do *you* acknowledge those who have helped you?

Zig Ziglar said, "If you give people what *they* want, you will automatically get what you want."

Take care of the needs of your wingmen, be they your customers, coworkers, or family members, and they'll be there for you. But don't wait to build those relationships and walk the flight line until you really need them, because it just might be too late. Elizabeth Dole, former head of the Red Cross, put it this way: "I didn't wait for the floods to come before I built relationships."

Walking the flight line is the core tenet of wingmanship, and it's one of the most essential practices you can adopt to build trust and credibility as a leader and wingman. When you take the time to learn about your peers and associates on both a professional and a personal level and then do your best to help them succeed, you transform a relationship into a partnership. Not only will you be able to work together to handle challenges and problems, but you'll also be much more effective at spotting and stopping those missile launches before they even leave the ground. And your wingmen will naturally want to celebrate their victories with you as well.

WALDO'S WINGTIP

Commander's Call

Sometimes it can be very difficult for a commander to get out and visit all the troops when information needs to be disseminated. So at least once a month, the squadron commander of a fighter squadron shuts down all operations and calls all wingmen (pilots, maintenance crew, administrators, technicians, and other crew) together for a meeting. The purpose of the meeting is to disseminate important information to the entire squadron and keep members aware of key updates, deployments, hot topics, and other important information. The commander also introduces new members of the squadron and bids farewell to those who are departing (either moving on to other assignments or retiring). Finally, awards are given out to the top quarterly (or annual) performers in all areas of operation: Instructor Pilot of the Quarter, Crew Chief of the Year, Maintenance Technician of the Year, and so forth. It's a great opportunity both to gauge and to stimulate morale and to reinforce the understanding that we're all members of the same unified team.

Regardless of your job description, you should gather your mission-critical wingmen at least once a month and let them hear news (good or bad) from you. Openly reward your top performers, and let everyone see that you appreciate their efforts. If you don't have a quarterly awards program, create a simple one—don't wait till the end of the year to reward your "top guns." These meetings should be fun, so don't let them devolve into gripe sessions. Allow guest speakers to share interesting content if time permits, but above all, keep the meetings creative and interactive, and always end them on a high note.

11

New Day, New Jet

Fail with Honor, and Bounce Back from Adversity

I DIDN'T FLIP the switch. It was as simple as that.

We all have our unflipped switches in business—things we forget to do, mistakes we make, deals we don't close because of something dumb we did, and straight-up bad decisions we made—but this one was a whopper. The little switch in question had put my entire flying career in jeopardy, and now I was suddenly down to my final shot at becoming a fighter pilot in the United States Air Force.

How could I have been so stupid? I had rehearsed the move a hundred times, but when I lifted that T-37 jet trainer off the ground and raised the gear handle, I left the landing lights down—a key mistake that cost me big-time.

If you exceed 135 knots with the landing lights deployed, you can damage them and cost the Air Force a few thousand dollars while the jet sits in the maintenance hangar awaiting repairs—not a good thing in an extremely busy flying squadron. My instructor pilot (IP), Capt. Scott Perko, caught the error, took control of the jet, and raised the lights himself. Here's the kicker: if an IP takes the jet from a trainee on a check ride, it's basically an instant bust—you failed the flight.

Unfortunately, this was the second flight in a row that Captain Perko had to take over because of my failure to raise those darned lights. And suddenly I was one step closer to washing out of undergraduate pilot training (UPT) and seeing my life's dream vanish in an instant.

At twenty-two years old, I was beginning to see this simple little mistake as one of the biggest tragedies of my young life. My failure to flip one little switch left me standing at the crossroads of my future. With my confidence at its lowest point and doubt pulsing through my veins, I asked myself, "What now?"

I had one last ride coming. This time, it was with my flight commander, Maj. Jerry Free. A combat-decorated former F-4 fighter pilot, he looked more Superman than military officer. Standing over six feet tall, in an impeccable uniform and in better shape than most officers my age, Major Free was sharp, charismatic, and a great pilot—the epitome of an Air Force officer. But he was also stern and demanding and did not tolerate slackers. He was intimidating, especially for a brand-new lieutenant going through the first (and most challenging) training program of his career.

In the pre-mission briefing room, expecting the worst, I fidgeted nervously with my checklist while waiting for Major Free to arrive. What if I did the unthinkable and did not raise the lights *again*? What if I messed up something else on the flight? What was I going to do if I washed out of UPT? What would I tell my family and friends—the people who seemed to have more confidence in me than I had in myself?

Every fear and self-doubt I could conjure up swirled through my head. I imagined my commander coming down on me hard: *"All right, Lieutenant Waldman, you mess up one more time and you're history!"*

That's when it happened.

Major Free walked into the room and sized me up. I stood at attention, braced myself, and saluted smartly.

"OK, Waldo," he said, "it's a new day, new jet. Are you ready to pass this flight, or what?"

He smiled and reached out to shake my hand.

At that moment, I could sense the energy in the room shift. Suddenly, everything changed. At least, in my head it did. I went from intimidation to inspiration, and a sensation of relief traveled from my head to my toes. All that stress and anxiety I had bottled up exploded out of me like a bullet and transformed itself into a shot of adrenaline. I could have knocked over a brick wall or run a marathon in the combat boots I was wearing.

New day, new jet. Wow. I had never heard that expression before. But somehow, those four words, and the man speaking them, changed my attitude from fear to focus just like that.

Major Free knew I was nervous, fearful, and full of doubt. He had seen it before with hundreds of young officers like me. The moment he walked into that briefing room, he could easily have given me the final nudge over the cliff of doubt where I stood and into the abyss of failure—a flightless path that would forever have defined me as someone who couldn't handle any pressure and couldn't perform because of his fears. I verged on becoming a man who had failed to reach a goal he wanted more than anything else in the world. But with those four words, "new day, new jet," I had a fresh start. My slate was wiped clean, and the past, with its glaring mistake, was yesterday's news.

Suddenly, I was back in business with the winning attitude that had landed me this opportunity in the first place.

I instantly stopped dwelling on my past mistake and the fact that one in three students washed out of UPT. Sure, I was still nervous and fearful. But now I started looking forward, reenergized and psyched about my new opportunity to excel. There was no way that I was going to let something as small as a landing-light switch take away my dream of becoming an Air Force pilot.

THE ONLY FAILURE IS NOT LEARNING FROM YOUR OWN MISTAKES

Past failure should not limit your future success. In fact, many times what we view as failures are really merely the prelude to victories over our fears.

In business, that's what it's all about: getting back up, looking optimistically ahead, facing doubt and fear head-on, and refusing to let the past determine our future. But it's also about those who help us get there, like Major Free, who was not about to let my mistake pull me down into a pit of despair.

Unfortunately, many of us live in an "old day, old jet" world. Living in the past, we allow our failures to poison the soil in which the seeds of our future growth are planted. We inadvertently spoil that soil with fear. Strapping into the old jet means the same fears will be with you on every mission, predisposing you toward making the same mistakes over and over again. More often than not, these life missions end in failure.

We all have limitations. Fear and self-doubt will somehow creep into our heads. Going into my check ride, I knew I would be fearful and nervous no matter how much I prepared. But I learned that the key is to get into a frame of mind where your focus is on *winning rather than on not losing*. Interesting distinction. To focus on *not failing*, you have to focus on failure, and this incites the fear that clouds our judgment and strangles our ability to take the right action. We wind up messing up and, in essence, "flipping the wrong switches."

We see this in business all the time. Fear and doubt creep in. Can I make the sale? Will I be rejected on this cold call? Will I be able to find another job? Am I going to meet my budget? Will my boss approve of the forecast? Instead of focusing on the win, we focus on what will happen if we fail. When we're caught in this vicious cycle, we wind up trying to take off with our brakes on, with the result that we can't execute with confidence and let our skills shine through.

When we *take our focus off the outcome* and instead focus on the moment that stands before us, we can face a challenge with power and confidence rather than fear.

I like to define how we handle fear in two ways: we can either Forget Everything And Run or Focus Energy and Accept Responsibility. Either way, the fear is still there, but in one response we are running away from it, and in the other we are walking straight into it. So how would you rather look at something scary in your life: from over your shoulder or facing it head-on?

In Chapter 9 we talked about deciding to abort a mission. While there are appropriate times to abort (as I did before the flight back to the United States from Spain), sometimes you have to buckle down, focus, and take action, especially when you're going for your dreams or trying to make something big happen in your business pursuits. For me, this was big—there was no way I was going to run away from getting my wings.

A LESSON FROM APPLE

When Steve Jobs cofounded Apple Computer, his visionary prowess allowed him to recruit one of the top executives in the business world at the time, Pepsi's John Sculley. Under Jobs's vision and Sculley's leadership, Apple, with its revolutionary graphical user interface and its game-changing use of "windows" (a concept that Bill Gates would eventually change the world with), started to establish itself as a real player in the computer industry.

But behind the scenes, the relationship wasn't going very well. Sculley and the other board members were becoming increasingly frustrated with Jobs's all-vision, no-leadership tendencies. Jobs thought his wingmen were covering his six and supporting him. They weren't. Instead, in one of the most talked-about coups in business history, Sculley and the board fired Jobs from the very company he created. Jobs faced a major failure before he could ever fully implement his full vision for Apple Computer.

But there's a happy ending to this story. Jobs dealt with the missiles and overcame the obstacles, and when Apple was in deep trouble in the mid-1990s, the board called him out of his exile and asked him to temporarily lead the company again. That temporary appointment turned into Jobs becoming the full-time CEO. And now, without the past failures and encumbrances in his way, he was able to take Apple to stratospheric new heights and reposition the company as one of the most innovative in the world today.

The Steve Jobs story teaches us that despite failure, there is always a new day, new jet, and that as long as you are still breathing, you can still regroup and take action again. Jobs failed his check ride with Apple, but because of his hard work, commitment, and refusal to call it quits, he still graduated with his wings and became CEO. He didn't give up. He knew in his heart what he was meant to do, and rather than run away and let his previous failure hold him back, he kept focused on his dream.

WINNERS PUSH THEMSELVES WHILE PULLING OTHERS

If you've ever worked out with weights, you know the value of a spotter, especially with the bench press. A spotter keeps you safe and also helps you get in a few more reps. I've spotted a lot of friends, but there's one spot I'll never forget. My friend Mike Funaki, who was younger and stronger than I, had 225 pounds on the bench and was going through his reps. On the sixth rep, he started really needing help.

"C'mon, Mike," I urged. "Get strong. Up, up, up!"

I had my index fingers barely even touching the weight underneath. He cranked out another two reps! Then, on the eighth and final rep, I had to help him out quite a bit (and almost pulled my back in the process!). He really went all out.

"Great spot, Waldo!" he said. "You really made me work for those last few."

So I was sitting there thinking how cool it is for someone to get someone else to push beyond their limits. Mike obviously knew what it took to grow strength and muscles—he was in tremendous shape. For those first few reps, I didn't need to touch the bar; I gave him zero physical assistance. I just had to encourage him a little bit more to dig deep and give it his all. With my encouraging words and, most important, the knowledge that I was there if his strength should fail him, he battled through a few more reps. And then, when he truly needed my help, he took a risk and went for one more rep—a rep he would never have attempted on his own. But with me there, he gave it a shot. I didn't push him. But on that last rep, I had to *pull* the weight up to let him complete the rep safely.

Wingmen never push. *They pull while inspiring others to push themselves to break their barriers.* When you have a trusted wingman by your side to catch you if you fail, you will take more risks and push yourself beyond where you think you can go. This, my friend, is where the growth is—in muscle strength and in life.

COMRADES OF COURAGE

Having a "new day, new jet" mentality isn't easy, just as it isn't easy hitting the weights in the gym or getting out of your comfort zone at work to conquer the project that will get you that promotion. I wish I always had the strength to transform my fear into focus and break through the barriers that hold me back from achieving my goals—to "push it up" on life's throttle *every* time. Failing is tough, especially if you try to fly solo. Often, we need other people to inspire us to push past our fears or weaknesses, because there is only so much we can do on our own. These people are our comrades of courage, those we can go to for help, a bit of encouragement, or even a jolt of adrenaline. Maj. Jerry Free was that person for me. He pulled me out of the pit I was in and showed me what I could do.

The day I took off with Major Free on my make-or-break flight, great things happened. There were so many areas where I could have messed up. *Never mind the landing lights*, I thought to myself. My power-on stalls, landings, and spin-recovery skills were just as critical. I couldn't afford to be stressed about my landing lights, because that would limit my ability to execute all the other maneuvers successfully.

During maneuvers, Major Free brought out the joy in what we were doing: flying freely in open sky in a high-performance jet. I'll never forget when, without warning, he took control of the aircraft and simulated a dive-bombing run on a cloud.

"Woo-hoo!" he howled. "Let's hit the target, Waldo!" he said as he rolled us inverted and dived toward the white puffs. The sheer exhilaration we felt at twenty thousand feet really got my blood pumping, but it also put me at ease. I was thrilled and remembered what I had so loved about flying in the first place. Suddenly, my focus shifted from my fear of failure to where it really needed to be: in the moment.

But Major Free didn't stop there. "OK, Waldo," he said, "you ready to do some power-on stalls? Show me how it's done," he challenged.

I grabbed the aircraft and flew like Chuck Yeager.

Like the little engine that could, I had someone who believed in me, and this made me believe in myself. He got me jazzed, and I went from "I think I can" to "I *know* I can."

I have discovered in my life experiences as a combat fighter pilot and as someone working in the competitive world of business that friends, partners, or colleagues—our wingmen—are the ones who can inspire us to take action even when we feel we can't. These wingmen not only motivate us, they *activate* us. They get us to push through a few more reps when the barbells of life seem too heavy!

A "new day, new jet" wingman brings these intentions into the game, into the fight—and as a good wingman, you'll do the same:

- "I'm not interested in what you did last time—I want to see what you can do *now*."
- "Your win is my win."
- "I'm your biggest cheerleader."
- "I will hold you accountable."
- "I will encourage you to improve."
- "I am here, and I will spot you when you need it."
- "I am not about to let you fail!"

Maj. Jerry Free was my true wingman on that crucial day. He held the keys to my future in his hands, but he also said to me loud and clear, "I believe in you. Now, go and take off!"

THE BEST WAY TO FIND WINGMEN IS TO BE ONE

Of course, mistakes are inevitable. But what really counts is what you do about them and how your wingmen help you overcome them on a new day, with a new jet. Through combat missions, claustrophobia, moving from the military to the business world, and starting my own company, there were times when I didn't think I would make it. And yet, in my journey, I had people who helped inspire and motivate me along the way. These key wingmen, like Major Free, always seemed to appear at just the right moment.

Make no mistake: if I hadn't performed to standard, Major Free had an obligation to fail me. But the failure was literally in my hands. Major Free didn't fly my jet for me, but he put me in a state of mind that blew out the cobwebs of fear and allowed me to perform to my full potential.

I earned a passing grade on that check ride thanks to the words "new day, new jet" and the wingman who delivered them. A few months later, I earned my wings and graduated from UPT. And now I'm challenging you to be the "Major Free" in someone else's life. Be the wingman who enlightens and inspires, who "Frees" people from their limitations and helps them find the courage to take action and to see their limitless possibilities.

The power of this journey we are on is in recognizing the freedom we gain when we wake up each day with a "new day, new jet" mentality. Every new day there's a new jet. Now, go fly it.

WALDO'S WINGTIP

Write down the names of the top five wingmen who are your encouragers in your life. Keep them on a checklist (maybe even put them right up on your refrigerator) to call when you're overwhelmed, experiencing a stall, or losing altitude. They can help shake you loose from the inertia of yesterday's lackluster performance so you can strap into a new jet on a new day. Do something special to thank them for being so supportive. Make it personal. The best way to thank these wingmen, however, is to then reach out to a wingman (or even someone you don't even know that well) who may be experiencing some turbulence and needs his or her spirit lifted. Give unconditionally without expecting something in return. Go out of your way to be a comrade of courage.

12

Service Before Self

Lend a Wing to Help Others Fly

As a PILOT in the 79th Fighter Squadron "Tigers" at Shaw Air Force Base, South Carolina, I was assigned to be chief of training and life support. Every fighter pilot in a fighter squadron has an additional duty other than flying, and this was mine. I was responsible for ensuring that the squadron's fifty pilots were up to speed with all facets of their training and that their equipment functioned perfectly. Since we were the most widely deployed squadron in the Air Force at the time, this was a critical and extremely demanding job. Fortunately, I had a wingman. His name was Sgt. Roy Summers, and I was his boss.

A technical sergeant with approximately fifteen years of service, Sergeant Summers was not an extraordinary soldier, nor was he a standout performer. Quiet and reserved, he opted to stay out of the spotlight. But when a job had to be done and done right, Sergeant Summers was the man. An amazingly hard worker, he knew how to inspect equipment and flight gear like no one else. He was a pro, and I depended on him to check my six and make sure the 79th was always in combat-ready status. We developed a great professional relationship, and I trusted Sergeant Summers completely.

Yet, like all of us, he had some issues. A heavy smoker who rarely hit the gym, he often worked through lunch on a Snickers bar and a Coke. His poor diet and lack of exercise caused him to gain some weight, and to maintain Air Force standards, I had to put him on a health and fitness program. No counseling, not even a discussion. I just ordered him to the health and wellness center and told him to check back in with me in a month.

Mission accomplished. Or so I thought.

A week later I got a phone call from my squadron. Sergeant Summers had suffered a stroke and was in the hospital. Although he was conscious and able to see, it was very serious.

I remember distinctly the first thought that went through my mind. It wasn't about Sergeant Summers and what he must be going through; it was that I just lost the most important wingman in my office. We were deploying in a few weeks, and now I was going to be undermanned. I thought to myself: *Because Sergeant Summers lacked the discipline and motivation to take care of himself, the rest of the squadron will have to suffer the consequences. And I am going to have to deal with it.*

When I arrived to the squadron, my commander told me that as his supervisor I should go visit Sergeant Summers in the hospital. Now I became even more frustrated, because I was scheduled to fly that morning, and I would have to take myself off the schedule. Reluctantly, I jumped into my car and arrived fifteen minutes later at the hospital in Sumter, South

Carolina. I checked in and made my way to Sergeant Summers's room. With every step, things started to change.

I couldn't remember the last time I had been in a hospital, and it felt uncomfortable and awkward. I breathed in the disinfectant-scented hospital air and gazed at the shiny hospital floor. I watched the faces of the people walking by me. Most were depressed and sullen, and I wondered what family member or friend they were visiting or who might be suffering. Perhaps their mom was recovering from radiation treatment or their friend was in a bad car wreck the night before. I started to really feel for these people.

Finally, I began to slow down, and the gravity of the situation became apparent as I began to think about Sergeant Summers. Though I was thirty-one years old, I had never known anyone who suffered a stroke. Would he live? How serious was it? Would he even be able to walk or talk? What about his career in the Air Force? What was his family going through?

I got very nervous. As I arrived at his room, I could feel my heart pounding away. What should I say? What could I possibly do to help him out?

I opened the door and found his bed surrounded by his wife, two children, and a few of his crew from the life support shop. It looked as if each of them had a hand on a part of his body. He was connected to a bunch of tubes and leads. The poor guy looked pathetic. My heart dropped.

"Sergeant Summers!" I called out instinctively. I saw his head lift up a little bit, and I walked up to the bed and put my hand on his shoulder. He was awake, but the entire left side of his body was slack and unmoving.

"How ya doing, Sergeant Summers?"

His eyes brightened, and he tried to talk, but all he could do was mumble. He was quite excited, and the words ran from his mouth, but I couldn't understand a thing. His wife was crying.

What should I say to this man who was in such an awful state? I firmly gripped his arm, and I said the first thing that came to my mind, "I'm proud of you, Sergeant Summers."

I wanted to let him know that despite his condition, despite how scared he must be, I was proud of him for fighting this like a man. If it were me in his place, I'm not sure how I would react. He needed some serious encouragement.

"Sergeant Summers, you better get well quick!" I said eagerly. "We're deploying in three weeks, and the squadron needs you. *I* need you! Can you do that for me?" I wanted to let him know he was still needed. I wanted to give him something to fight for.

He got even more excited and was apparently trying to explain something to me. He continued mumbling uncontrollably, and I had no idea what he was saying. And that's when the tears started streaming down his face. My heart broke for him, and there was nothing I could do.

I knew very well that his chances of wearing his Air Force uniform again and serving his country were close to zero, and I think he knew it, too. His life was forever changed.

And then I felt ashamed. I realized what a terrible wingman I had been to him. A man with a family and a life, with hopes and dreams, was suffering, and all I cared about was myself, my job, and not looking bad in front of my squadron. I was upset about not being able to fly that day, but here was someone who might not even be able to *walk* again. I didn't have a clue about leadership.

Sergeant Summers worked for me. He was my wingman, but I treated him like a stranger. When he was working those long hours in the back office, I never asked him how things were going. I never inquired about his family or his personal life or if he had any health issues that were concerning him. Why was he spending so much time at work and never taking lunch? Why was he smoking two packs a day and putting on weight? Was there something going on that I wasn't aware of? Instead of really connecting with him like a true wingman, I barked orders at him and never really thought about what I could do to help him deal with his issues. I did the easy thing: I put him on probation and stuck him on a fitness program. I expected him to serve me, but I never served him.

I was his boss, but I wasn't his wingman.

THE MISSION OF SERVICE

What I learned that day was that to make a difference as a wingman, you have to go above and beyond. I wasn't doing enough.

To me, the mission was about getting the job done in the life support shop. It was not about the people. Sergeant Summers had a mission, but I didn't know about it, because I never asked. I needed him, and so did the squadron, but he had another mission. He had a life outside that life support shop. Watching him in his hospital bed that day, I realized that his mission, now more than ever, was his wife and kids who stood by his side.

"Service before self" is one of three core values of the Air Force. They are called the armed *services* for a reason. And service always involves sacrifice in some way. It means giving something.

When people are in trouble or experiencing a challenge in life, they may not have the courage to ask for help. They may not even know they *need* help. This is why a good wingman always checks the six of those around him: to protect their blind spots. A good wingman takes himself off the flying schedule and sacrifices the day to give support and hope to someone whose wings have been clipped or damaged. A good wingman goes the extra mile and pushes it up by spending the time with a coworker in need, perhaps even going so far as to have a meaningful conversation. A good wingman is always willing to give someone a battle-damage check, to see if he's OK. A good wingman lifts others up rather than dragging them down.

In March 1967, a combat mission flown by two Air Force F-4 fighter pilots in North Vietnam demonstrated the true meaning of service before self. Capt. Bob Pardo was the flight lead, and his wingman was Capt. Earl Aman. Both were hit by antiaircraft artillery and had damage to their aircraft. Aman's fuel tanks were badly damaged and he lost most of his fuel, which eliminated his chances of reaching the airborne tanker to refuel. Rather than watch his helpless wingman eject over enemy territory and risk capture, Pardo put his own aircraft (and his own life) in danger to help him.

After ordering Aman to shut down his engines, Pardo maneuvered the nose of his aircraft under the tailhook of Aman's jet and literally pushed it to keep it airborne and slow its rate of descent. Despite having only one engine of his own operating (he had to shut the other down because of a fire) and despite a cracking windshield (from the tremendous structural stress of pushing Aman's jet), Pardo continued to put his life in danger to help his wingman. With the slightest mistake, the tailhook could have broken the one-inch-thick glass canopy and crushed him. Fortunately, Pardo was able to keep pushing until he had the two jets in friendly airspace, avoiding enemy forces, at which time both pilots bailed out and were eventually rescued.[1]

NEVER LEAVE YOUR WINGMAN BEHIND

What an amazing story of wingmanship. This is how we serve above all. I have to admit that in combat there were times when I wasn't flying for my country. Believe me, I doubt that Pardo and Aman were thinking of their country, either, during their emergency. What you think about is taking care of your buddy and making sure you all get home alive. You never leave a wingman behind.

Imagine if everyone in the armed services turned around and ran when their wingmen needed help. Now imagine how cohesive your organization would be if it were filled with dedicated, service-oriented wingmen like Pardo.

Who in your squadron may be running out of fuel and looking for help? Are you turning a blind eye, or are you extending one of your wings in service? Today it may be someone else who needs help, but who's to say that tomorrow it couldn't be you? Sometimes the tiniest gesture of kindness can make all the difference to someone who is hurting inside. After all, you don't know what's going on in the mind or the life of the wingman in the cubicle next to you. Maybe her spouse is out of work, his child is ill, or her 401(k) account is in a free-fall. You just never know. But a wingman goes above and beyond.

---

1. John L. Frisbee, "Valor: Pardo's Push," *Air Force Magazine*, October 1996, www .airforce-magazine.com/MagazineArchive/Pages/1996/October%201996/1096 valor.aspx.

MAKE A DIFFERENCE

The Ritz-Carlton hotel chain has a great mission statement: "Ladies and gentlemen serving ladies and gentlemen." Crisp, clear, and to the point. They ask themselves two questions every day:

- What did we learn from yesterday?
- What can we do *today* to make a difference for our customer?

The past is over; the future hasn't happened. We need to think about what we can do *today* to make a difference for those who walk through the doors of our lives and request service. What can you do today to make a difference?

I could have done something more the day I found out that Sergeant Summers had a problem. I could have done a better job connecting, or I could have led like Psycho, but I didn't. Psycho showed me the meaning of service when he acknowledged my being tardy. He cared beyond the job responsibility I had. He was my commander, but he knew that for me to serve him and the mission of the squadron, he needed to set an example by serving me. But it was more than that: Psycho was a genuinely humble guy who valued people, and he knew how to serve.

Constantly asking yourself three questions will keep you focused on service every day. Remember them, remind your wingmen of them, and ask your wingmen to remind you:

- Who needs me now?
- How can I help now?
- What would I want if I were the person in need?

I believe we are all wired by our creator to serve. When people call out Mayday to us, it's almost impossible not to help them, especially if they are business associates, close friends, or family. By constantly asking yourself these three questions, you will keep yourself in a serving state of mind—thinking about, and looking for, opportunities to serve. Imagine what can happen when an entire working group of people is focused on serving each other.

On the ladder of life, we need to have one hand reaching up to a wingman who will pull us up to the next rung of success. And we also need to have one hand reaching down to help lift someone else up to the next rung. And sometimes, like Pardo, we need to push our wingmen when they're out of fuel and have no thrust of their own to finish the mission.

The first four words of Rick Warren's *The Purpose-Driven Life* are profound: "It's not about you." He's right, of course. True happiness in life comes from serving others. But that doesn't mean that we can—or even should—devote ourselves to others 100 percent of the time. It's simply not the way human beings were meant to work. We can't help anyone if we aren't taking care of ourselves as we go.

We've all known people who spent all their time and energy taking care of everyone else but were meanwhile neglecting themselves. They give and give, and in the end they become resentful because no one was looking out for *them*. The thing is, no one else was *supposed* to be looking out for them—that was *their* job, not someone else's. Have you been there? I know I have! Sometimes it needs to be about ourselves. We need to take care of and serve our inner wingman before we can serve another. That isn't being selfish; it's being reasonable and responsible.

I challenge you to examine your life for the places you've been neglecting yourself, and when you find them, take the time to serve yourself and refuel. Give yourself a break. Learn to say no; then take that day off and relax by the pool, take a hike in the woods, or curl up with a book. Take the time to be generous with yourself as well as others. In the end, you'll find yourself more fulfilled and at peace in your own life, and that will give you the added thrust to help others on their flight path.

WALDO'S WINGTIP

Serve More with Less

In these economically trying times, we hear a lot about the need to "do more with less." Good advice, but why not up the ante and *give* more with less? Serve at a soup kitchen, visit a local hospital, mentor a teenager with no parents, donate to a local charity, or help out a veteran with a broken wing. When you see someone who is struggling and losing altitude, don't turn a blind eye and lose sight of what really matters in life. Use your wings to give them a lift and even a push if necessary. Sometimes all a flyer needs to stay airborne is just a little bit of encouragement and support. Let them know you've got their back and won't let them crash. Be the wind beneath their wings. Giving is winning.

13

Release Brakes!

Conquer the Fear Barrier That Holds You Back

THE FLASHING TAXI lights reflect off my canopy and light up my cockpit with a warm glow. It's eleven P.M., and the moonless sky is blanketed with stars—a beautiful night to fly. Waiting nervously for the tower's clearance to take off, I silently review the departure procedures in my head. The mission has been briefed, and the objectives are clear. I've already "chair flown" the mission a dozen times in my head. I know by heart the tactics, radio calls, and threat-reaction procedures to defeat the missiles that will soon saturate the airspace we will be navigating.

I look to my left and right and see the three other members of my formation. Yoda, the four-ship flight lead, is to my left. To my right are Pigpen and Shooter. We've trained together for this mission, and now it's time to execute. I'm filled with courage and confidence, knowing I won't be flying solo. We are one team, one mission. We are wingmen.

The radio call from the tower comes through my headset. "Viper flight, taxi into position and hold."

I clamp the oxygen mask down over my face and run up the throttle as I take my position on the runway. As usual, my heartbeat ramps up and my mouth starts to feel dry. I gaze down the runway and miles away, out into the night sky. I'll be up in that black hole for six hours tonight.

It feels like an eternity, but the call finally comes. "Viper flight, cleared for takeoff."

It's go time.

Yoda is first. I watch as his engine kicks into afterburner and brightens the runway all around him. The sound is deafening. In an instant, he's blasting down the runway, and I watch him lift off. Now it's my turn.

My left hand engages the throttle as I crank the engine to full military power while compressing the rudder pedals down to engage my brakes. The plane is shaking as I scan my engine instruments. All "check good." My heart is pounding. I look down at the photo of my niece and nephew, kiss the angel wings on my checklist, and then push it up to max afterburner. Releasing the brakes, I am slung back into my seat as the jet accelerates down the runway.

There's no turning back. I'm committed to this mission. I'm free.

That night, I "broke right" and defeated four surface-to-air missiles, lost sight of my flight lead, overcame vertigo on the tanker, and battled a claustrophobic panic attack headed home from the tanker. It was the most intense mission of my life. But I survived.

Actually, I did more than survive—I won. Along with my wingmen, I came back to a hot cappuccino, a squadron of friends, and a feeling of accomplishment that simply cannot be put in words. I defeated the demons that grabbed and clawed and tried to hold me back, and proved I was capable of breaking through my fear barrier and achieving victory.

All this happened because I had the courage to release my brakes and take off.

You may be strapped into your aircraft, mission-ready and cleared for takeoff. You've pushed up your engine to max power, and all your instruments "check good." You're prepared, have a team of wingmen to support you, and are committed to success. You're just waiting to find the courage to release your brakes.

My wingman, it doesn't make a difference how prepared you are, who is on your team, or how committed you are to success. Unless you take action and release the brakes on your life, you will never be able to conquer the barriers holding you back from reaching new heights. This is ultimately where the key to success lies.

TAKE ACTION

If "Push it up!" is the commitment of a wingman, "Release brakes!" is the action. *True commitment exists only when it is aligned with action.* Action based on disciplined preparation, laser focus, and, most of all, courage. The sort of courage that says, "Even though I may get shot at, I will carry on." This is the reality of flying fighters in combat, and the reality of winning in any arena of business.

So what are you committed to? Are you willing to take action to achieve it?

Attitude alone won't get your career off the ground. Yes, it's important, but for change to occur, ultimately you have to take action. A "push it up" attitude gives the thrust, but action provides the vector. You have to release the brakes on your jet and roll down the runway with a *target and a plan*, knowing full well what the stakes are. It can be overwhelming, and it is never easy. But the greatest results require the greatest risk and effort.

FEAR OR LEAD

We all know someone who recently lost a job or whose business is struggling. Maybe it's you. Business can be tough. Sales sometimes drop, budgets get slashed, and jobs are cut. When this happens, we all are affected. And while you can't always control everything in your work life, you can control *how you react* to what is happening. An old friend of mine once told me, when adversity strikes, "You either fear or lead."

If you fear, you *crawl* out of bed, anxious and worried, and focus on what you don't have. You become strangled with doubt. You strap into your jet ready to take off, but then push up the throttle with the brakes on. Doubt keeps your foot on the brakes and destroys the warrior spirit. It kills performance, which inevitably leads to failure.

If you lead, you *jump* out of bed, acknowledge your fear (it's normal to be afraid when adversity looms), and then *give thanks* for what you have. You marshal your resources, plan the day's mission, and take action. You focus on doing, not doubting—on performance, not philosophy. You understand that you are in control of your jet and are ultimately responsible for getting it to the target and back.

As I mentioned before, attitude alone does not determine altitude. Attitude *plus action* determines altitude!

The world rewards *action*, not attitude.

When adverse conditions arise, you have to ask yourself, *will I fear or lead?* In turbulent times, when the missiles are headed your way, it's time to *be a warrior, not a worrier.*

THE WARRIOR SPIRIT

Warriors acknowledge the reality of their fears and then lead by action. When I flew in combat with my wingmen, sure, we were scared! Sure, we had doubts. But when it came time to execute, we had already prepared relentlessly as a team, and now we took action as a team. We felt confident because we were not flying solo and knew we could count on each other for mutual support. Most important, we focused on our actions, not our attitude.

Being a modern-day warrior is not about combat. Warriors live by the credo "The more you sweat in peace, the less you bleed in battle." They plan and train with discipline and intensity and put forth the effort so that they never have to go to battle. As the great Chinese military strategist Sun Tzu wrote in *The Art of War*, "The greatest victories in war are the ones that are never fought."

Warriors are also the consummate wingmen, who will do what it takes to help you turn your fear into courage, push up your throttle, release your brakes, and take off. Warriors want their wingmen to win.

FLY OUTSIDE YOUR COMFORT ZONE

At some point while reading this book, you have probably wondered why, knowing that I was phobic about enclosed spaces *and* heights, I chose to fly the F-16. Before I flew fighters, I was an Air Force instructor pilot, teaching men and women how to fly. It was fun and fairly easy—hour-long flights over friendly airspace, with no missiles or night refueling. Despite the rare panic attack when flying cross country or in bad weather, I enjoyed the job and earned "instructor pilot of the year" awards and lots of great recognition. I was a success, not necessarily because I was a good pilot but because I worked really hard, focused on my students, and took instructing very seriously. I simply loved to teach and inspire my students to be the best.

When it came time to move on to my next assignment, I was allowed to fly any aircraft I wanted. This made the choice even tougher. I could fly the new C-17 cargo plane on nine-hour hauls to Africa and Europe—big, roomy cockpits, box lunches, and boredom. Or, I could fly the F-16, one of the most amazing jets of the modern day—Mach 2, weapons and sensors, nine Gs, deployments to remote locations, six-hour night combat missions, and a tiny, cramped cockpit.

You obviously know which aircraft I chose.

Why? Because I didn't want to play it safe. I didn't want to look back on my life and tell my children I had a chance to fly the coolest jet in the world but instead sold out to my fear, played it safe, and let somebody else have all the fun.

Making that tough choice released the brakes on my commitment to live a challenging, exciting, *full* life. If I hadn't made that choice, I wouldn't have had the amazing life experiences, trials and tribulations that helped create the content of this book you now hold in your hands. I would have always wondered what it would have been like to experience the thrill and challenge of flying a jet fighter.

This much I have learned: when you look back on your life, it's usually not things you *did* that you regret; it's the things you *didn't* do.

Sometimes you have to step outside your comfort zone and take a risk in order to grow. If you're satisfied with where you are right now, that's terrific! If you're a success and living a full life, more power to you! But I'm talking about reaching *new* heights in your life and not settling for the status quo. This is about stepping outside the comfort zone of your cockpit and doing what it takes to break the performance barrier that, ultimately, is constructed out of nothing but your own invented fears. This is how you take your life and your career to the next level.

The Opposite Side of Fear Is Growth

The greater the fear, the greater the opportunity for growth.

If you're scared and anxious about leaving your job, starting a new business, taking that promotion, or moving overseas, that is a sign that you are on to something great in your life. I'm not saying you must take the action that is making you fearful. But it really is worth taking a close look at, because behind this fear is opportunity.

Courage Isn't Fearlessness

Don't be fearless. For one thing, it's impossible. Just strive to be courageous. Acknowledge your fear and use it as a tool to really explore what it is you want (or don't want) in life. Courage inspires action, which leads to performance beyond your old limits, which results in joy unlike any other.

I will leave you with one final story that epitomizes my release from fear and a change in the trajectory of my life.

FLYING SOLO

My presolo ride was terrible. As we taxied the Cessna T-41 preliminary trainer back to the flight line, all I could think about was how badly I had blown it. It was my first chance to show my instructor pilot, Capt. Bob Massarella, that I was ready to fly on my own. It was a traffic-pattern-only flight, and I was all over the place. My airspeeds were fast, my altitude was consistently a hundred feet off, and my glide path on final approach to the runway was too steep, almost to the point of being dangerous.

We taxied back to the hangar in silence. I had messed up, and Captain Massarella and I both knew it. I had only two more shots to qualify for solo, or it was over—I would wash out of preliminary flight training and never even make it to jet training after graduating from the Air Force Academy. I was deflated and angry with myself.

As we began to pull into the hangar, Captain Massarella barked, "Stop the aircraft!"

Alarmed, I pulled the throttle back to idle and hammered down on the brakes. "What's up, sir?" I asked.

Then he began to unstrap from his seat. I looked at him in utter bewilderment and asked, "What are you doing?"

"Waldo, I'm getting out of this aircraft, and you're going solo. If you want to kill yourself, that's fine with me, but I am not going to be in the plane when it happens."

In an instant, he had jumped out of the plane, slammed the door behind him, and was standing on the tarmac giving me a thumbs-up. He smiled. "You can do it, Waldo!" he yelled out. And before I could get a word out, he was gone.

What the hell! I thought. *I'm not ready for this!*

There I was, by myself in this plane with no one there to help me. All I could hear was the steady rumble of the prop engine, and my breath over the intercom. I was supposed to go solo . . . *right now.* With that, I began to panic. My legs started shaking uncontrollably. My mouth became parched. I started to freak out. How the heck was I going to *do* this? I had just flown the worst takeoffs and landings of my life, and now I was expected to go solo? What if I crashed?

I couldn't taxi back and shut down—Captain Massarella would have my head. I couldn't let him down. Besides, my fellow cadets would really think I was pathetic. If I quit today, I wouldn't be able to face them. I had to dig deep, right now, and find the courage to press on with the mission.

I taxied the T-41 to the runway and ran through my pre-departure checklists: flaps, radios, altimeter . . . set. I checked and rechecked everything. I could not believe I was going solo.

I called to the tower on the radio: "Cessna fifteen, ready for takeoff."

"Cessna fifteen, altimeter setting is 29.92. Cleared for takeoff, runway one six right."

I added 80 percent power to the throttle and hammered down on the brake pedals while checking the engine instruments. My hands and legs were still shaking. It was time to take off. I wanted to close my eyes.

Those five seconds before takeoff seemed an eternity; then I finally released the brake pedals and accelerated down the runway, and within seconds I lifted off. *Confirm good climbing indications, gear handle up, flaps up.*

I was flying!

My fear and panic suddenly disappeared as I became totally engrossed in the moment. I was never so completely focused in my life. I scanned every instrument, cross-checked my altitude and airspeed, and monitored my displacement from the runway like a seasoned instructor with two thousand hours of flight time. No deviations. My final turn and approach were nearly flawless as I corrected my glide path and made sure my aim point was set in the first two hundred feet of the runway . . . just like I chair flew. I had never flown this well before. If Captain Massarella were with me now, man, would he be impressed!

I flew around four touch-and-gos, landed, and taxied back to the hangar, where I was greeted by a very pleased instructor.

"Amazing job, Waldo—I knew you could do it!" he yelled. A great bear hug followed.

That initial solo flight in the clunky old Cessna was probably the most exciting moment of my eleven-year flying career. Yes, I was flying by myself. But I wasn't flying solo. Captain Massarella was up there with me.

Looking back, I realized that the toughest part of going solo was not the flying—it was having the courage to release those brakes and take off. Once I did, my training took over and my fear dissipated. I became absorbed in the moment, freed of all extraneous obstacles, and engaged in the process of flying—I was fully present. I was alive.

If it were up to me, I would have never taken off. But Captain Massarella gave me wings to fly.

Many of us have an intense desire to take bold new action in our lives but never do for fear of failure. We are essentially pouring on the power with the brakes still applied. Consciously or subconsciously, we sabotage our success by living life with our foot on the brakes.

Releasing those brakes and simply going for it is how we grow in our personal and professional relationships. Captain Massarella, in his quirky, obnoxious, but loving manner, made me attack my fear demons. He knew I was better than I thought I was and was confident that I would rise to the occasion. He wanted me to succeed. He believed not only in my ability but in me.

He was my wingman.

THE GREATEST CHALLENGE IS LEAVING THE GROUND EACH DAY

I'm asking you, as you approach your work and handle the day-to-day missiles of business, to make the conscious choice to lead rather than fear. Be thankful for the warriors in your life who fight the good fight and give you the courage to release your brakes and take off in turbulent conditions. Ask for the strength to be a warrior for your customer, your coworkers, and those who aren't yet ready to release the brakes on their own.

Because nothing happens on the ground. For life to occur, you must get up in the air and flap your wings—that's where the growth is.

Releasing your brakes frees you to focus on what matters most. It's the first step on the journey to fulfillment, and it requires courage, preparation, and the support of your best wingmen.

Remember, fighter pilots aren't trained to hang out in the officers' club and look good—they are meant to fly. And so are you.

I want you to break whatever flight ceiling you have imposed on yourself. I want you to release the brakes and soar as you have never soared before. With your wingmen by your side, I want you to take flight, defeat the missiles, and create a courageous life built on the foundation of service and trust. You can and will fly higher, faster, and farther, because you are never flying solo.

Luciano De Crescenzo wrote, "We are each of us angels with only one wing. And we can only fly by embracing each other."

Those "angels" are your wingmen, and my wish for you is that on your flight through life, you always have them checking your six.

Push it up!

WALDO'S WINGTIP

Make a commitment today to go for something that you've been holding back from doing. It doesn't have to be something huge and fearsome. Rather, it should be an action that, deep down, you know you've been neglecting and should do. Perhaps it's taking a business course, joining Toastmasters, starting your own company, getting fit, putting in for a promotion, or learning to play the guitar. By taking small risks and succeeding, you will incrementally change your character and mind-set to take more and bigger risks. The inevitable result is growth and greater joy in life.

WINGMAN GLOSSARY OF TERMS

"Abort, abort!": The decision to quit a project, job, or relationship

Battle-damage check: An assessment of your wingmen to make sure they are OK to fly

Bingo: The point at which a mission must be aborted in order to return home before running out of fuel

Blind: When you've lost sight of your wingmen, coworker, or customer

Bling man: A wealthy and successful wingman

"Break right!": To call out threats and provide feedback to your wingmen

Chair flying: Mission rehearsing and planning for contingencies

Chase ship: A wingman who comes to the aid of a damaged or discouraged wingman

Check-in: Verbal connection with a wingman to check on his or her well-being

Checklist: A brief, easy-to-read, and step-by-step outline of a required list of action items

Check six: To cross-check your wingmen's most vulnerable position, their blind spot

Clear: No enemy or threat behind you is present (i.e., "your six is clear")

"Commit, commit!": A wingman's assertion that he or she will take action and release brakes

Engaged: The status of a wingman who is actively dealing with a challenge, customer, or important project (the opposite of supporting)

FEAR: Focus Energy, Accept Responsibility

Flight lead: The person in charge of leading a group of wingmen on a particular project

Flight plan: A step-by-step process to accomplish a mission or deal with a contingency

"I have the aircraft!": A statement of ownership of your mission and of being fully accountable for results

Lose sight, lose fight: A saying that means to keep sight of your wingmen and always find meaning in your mission

Lost wingman: Someone who lacks guidance or direction in his or her life

"Mayday, Mayday!": A distress call symbolizing the ability to call out for help to your wingmen

Mutual support: When two or more wingmen work together to provide open communication, encouragement, and mission-critical feedback

New day, new jet: A mind-set for bouncing back from failure and looking optimistically to the future

Over-G: A breach in one's integrity or moral compass

Push it up!: To apply maximum effort and commitment to a mission

Release brakes: To have the courage to take action despite your fear

Situational awareness: The ability to assess one's environment, threats, and wingmen

Status: Request for a wingman's situational awareness and position

Supporting: The act of assisting the engaged wingman while maintaining overall situational awareness

Task saturation: The inability to process extra information in the face of excessive workload (task overload)

Tumbleweed: A wingman who has lost situational awareness and direction in business or life

Walking the flight line: Connecting with your coworkers and getting to know them

Wing giver: A wingman who gives a wing away to help someone else fly

Wingman: A trusted partner in business and life

Wingmanship: The act of giving courage, mutual support, and assistance to others

Wing mom/Wing dad: Awesome parents who one can always go to for help

Wing nut: Someone who lacks trust (a wingman with a screw loose)

Wingworking: Networking with a focus on serving others

INDEX

ABOUT THE AUTHOR

Known as "the Wingman," Rob "Waldo" Waldman overcame a lifelong battle with claustrophobia and a fear of heights to become a decorated combat U.S. Air Force fighter pilot and highly successful businessman. He is a graduate of the U.S. Air Force Academy and also holds an M.B.A. with a focus on organizational behavior. After the military, he transitioned to the business world where he led national sales efforts for several companies before founding his own firm, Wingman Consulting.

Waldo teaches individuals and organizations how to build trusting relationships with their employees, partners, and customers. While relaying his personal experiences as a decorated combat fighter pilot and businessman, he makes striking parallels between the two that are memorable and exciting and brings "Top Gun" energy into each story and illustration.

Waldo's personal motto is "Winners Never Fly Solo," and he believes that the key to building a culture of trust lies with your wingmen—the men and women in your life who help you to overcome obstacles, adapt to change, and achieve success.

Audiences connect with him not only because of his extensive business background but also because he truly speaks from the heart and has an infectious passion for helping people. Waldo's captivating personal stories combined with dramatic jet fighter video footage and inspirational music will encourage you to prepare diligently for every mission, face challenges with courage, build more meaningful relationships, and maximize your potential both in business and in life.

Waldo's clients include Nokia, New York Life, Home Depot, Medtronic, and dozens of associations, health care companies, and educational institutions.

Learn more at www.yourwingman.com or call 1-866-925-3616.

Stay connected with Waldo on the Web:
www.twitter.com/waldowaldman
www.facebook.com/waldowaldman
www.linkedin.com/in/waldowaldman

SUPPORT OUR COUNTRY'S WINGMEN—OUR VETERANS

Each day when we hit the flight line of business, it's easy to take for granted the blessings and freedoms we all enjoy. Our country was built on the sweat and sacrifice of so many who came before us. It's important that we not forget those who dug the well of our freedom.

We also can't forget to honor those who sacrifice every day to keep our country free. The men and women who serve in uniform are wingmen not only to America but to the world. We need to honor and serve our veterans (past and present) and let them know we are their wingmen, too.

This is why a portion of the proceeds from the sale of this book will be donated to veterans' organizations. The nonprofits listed below are making a huge difference for our veterans and the communities they serve. Please take a moment to learn more about how these organizations are supporting our country's heroes and their families.

Wounded Warriors: Provides programs and services to severely injured service members during the time between their active duty and their transition to the civilian sector. Its mission is to honor and empower wounded warriors. **www.woundedwarriorproject.org**

The American Legion: The nation's most influential, effective, and dependable advocate for veteran affairs—from pushing for improved housing for active-duty families, to caring for the sick and wounded returning from Iraq and Afghanistan, to supporting community activities ranging from hospital services and blood drives to youth programs. **www.legion.org**

Tragedy Assistance Program for Survivors (TAPS): A community resource for those grieving the death of a loved one who served our country. Provides 24/7 comfort and care through comprehensive services and programs, including peer-based emotional support, casework assistance, crisis intervention, and grief and trauma resources. **www.taps.org**

BOOK THE WINGMAN TO SPEAK
and turn your next meeting into a Top Gun event!

Are you looking for a creative and exciting way to kick off or close your annual meeting or convention?

Are you ready for a hands-on leadership program that will help transform your organization into a cohesive team of mission-ready wingmen?

Waldo's high-energy, interactive keynotes and peak performance seminars engage the leadership, sales and customer service challenges faced by your organization today. Your team will strap into the cockpit of a high-performance jet and fly a mission on Waldo's wing as he shows you how you can adapt to change, build trusting relationships and take action that leads to results in business and life.

For a detailed list of Waldo's keynotes and seminars along with demo videos, visit **www.yourwingman.com,** e-mail **info@yourwingman.com,** or call **1-866-925-3616** and start planning your mission today.

WINGMAN FLIGHT PLAN FOR SUCCESS

What can you do to become a more **disciplined,
focused** and **courageous** leader
when facing change and adversity?

How can you instill a climate of ownership in
your organization so that every person feels they are
accountable and **responsible** for its success?

What tools can you employ to motivate
the members of your organization to
focus on the mission rather than themselves?

The Wingman Flight Plan for Success is a highly innovative leadership program that will teach you or your organization to become peak performance wingmen. Waldo and his team of Top Gun instructors bring the **Never Fly Solo** concepts to life through live, interactive seminars and online multimedia training.

– *Wingman Leadership Program (3 hours up to two full days)
Waldo and his wingmen will deploy to your organization and deliver hands-on interactive leadership training to create a culture of courage, accountability and excellence.*

– *Wingman Flight Plan Leadership Training Exercise
Online instructional module for the entrepreneur or corporate manager. This customizable program delivers highly effective, on-demand multimedia leadership training to help you or your team become more accountable and mission-ready wingmen.*

*For an on-line demo or to learn how to build a Flight Plan for Success and achieve "Wingman Flight Leader Certification," visit **www.yourwingman.com** or call **1-866-925-3616**.*

NEVER FLY SOLO RESOURCES AND WING GIFTS
To order, visit www.neverflysolo.com

Waldo's **Never Fly Solo** resources and wing gifts are a perfect way to reinforce the concepts of this book and express gratitude to colleagues, customers, employees or anyone who has helped make a difference in your business or life.

Wingman Coin
A customizable conference gift, they are a fun way to build team unity and serve as a unique reminder of your corporate values and mission.

T-Shirt
Show you are a trusted partner with a Never Fly Solo T-shirt!

Mug
Waldo's exclusive **"got wingmen?®"** *mug is a daily reminder to Never Fly Solo.*

Never Fly Solo Audio Keynote
Soar to new heights with the Wingman's high-energy, one-hour Never Fly Solo keynote program.

WingTips of the Week
Visit **www.yourwingman.com** and sign up for Waldo's weekly WingTips and keep the Never Fly Solo concepts top of mind.

WingTips Card
A quick reference card to remind you of the core principles of being a wingman in business and life.

Sales Mission Briefing Guide
A pre-mission sales call checklist to ensure you are mission-ready.